A Treasury of Texas Trivia II

T0159237

Bill Cannon

Republic of Texas Press
Plano, Texas

Library of Congress Cataloging-in-Publication Data

Cannon, Bill.
   A treasury of Texas trivia II / Bill Cannon.
      p.   cm.
   Includes index.
   ISBN 1-55622-699-3 (pbk.)
   1. Texas Miscellanea.   2. Texas Anecdotes.   I. Title.   II.   Title:
   Treasury of Texas trivia two.
   F386.6.C363   1999
   976.4—dc21   99-30025
                                                 CIP

Republic of Texas Press is an imprint of Wordware Publishing, Inc.
No part of this book may be reproduced in any form or by
any means without permission in writing from
Wordware Publishing, Inc.

Printed in the United States of America

ISBN 1-55622-699-3
10 9 8 7 6 5 4 3 2
9909

All inquiries for volume purchases of this book should be addressed to
Wordware Publishing, Inc., at 2320 Los Rios Boulevard, Plano, Texas 75074.
Telephone inquiries may be made by calling:

(972) 423-0090

Contents

Contents

Contents

Part III—Texas Family Secrets

Contents

Contents

Contents

Contents

Dedication

This book is dedicated to my wife, Marianne, without whose efforts my printed works would remain only a dream!

An old Texas saying is "If you see a turtle on a fence post, you can bet your boots someone helped him get there!" Marianne was that someone for me.

Acknowledgments

There is no better place than in the beginning of a book such as this to pay tribute to the people who were instrumental in bringing this collection of trivia items together. An enormous amount of research is required to ferret out and verify the facts surrounding each item of trivia selected for publication.

Because information comes from so many people and sources, it is difficult to acknowledge every helping hand without overlooking someone. To those whom I may inadvertently forget, I can only say, "excuse me!"

I am especially indebted to the Reference Department at the Irving Public Library and to the many libraries, large and small across the state that photocopied material and mailed it to me. I am equally indebted to the numerous Chambers of Commerce who helped me point out their cities in some small way.

Thanks to my wife, Marianne, who did much of the "nitty-gritty" work a book such as this requires. She came to my aid with such tasks I couldn't handle. She photographed many Texas scenes she never thought she would visit, I am sure.

The *Handbook of Texas* from the Texas State Historical Association was referred to daily while compiling my facts. I am indebted to *Texas Highways Magazine* for much inspiration toward further research.

I am extremely grateful to C.W. (Chet) Holliday for helping me come into the twentieth century by making me somewhat computer literate. It was a hard mountain for Chet to climb.

Introduction

In our first edition of *A Treasury of Texas Trivia* we wrote, "One thing that I most emphatically learned is that this book can never be finished. One can only take a breather." This acknowledgment has proved to be true. The book has resulted in many communications all bearing the same message in one form or another, "I wish you had included such and such an incident." The sender then referred to a particular fact or happening. These much-appreciated suggestions prompted additional research and verification. The research yielded more trivia items worth recording. These additional items of Texas trivia are bound together in this second edition of *A Treasury of Texas Trivia*.

Part I

Unusual Claims to Fame

*F*ame can sometimes be a fleeting thing unless firmly anchored. It is that to which fame is anchored that causes us to remember someone or something. For instance Boston has its "Tea Party," and San Antonio has its Alamo. As vast as Texas is, there are just not enough Alamos to go around! Yet many Texas towns and regions have gained lasting recognition in various ways, some of which seem quite unusual. Miles of Texas travel and volumes of Texas literature have yielded more than enough unusual claims to fame to devote a section of this book to.

Some of the most memorable and bizarre ones have found their way here. No doubt, readers can, with little thought, supply an equal number!

George B. "Machine-Gun" Kelly

One of America's most infamous characters of the 1930s put Wise County, Texas, in the headlines in 1933 when, prompted by his ambitious, excitement-craving wife, he kidnapped Oklahoma millionaire oilman Charles Urschel and held him for ransom on his wife's parents' ranch near the Wise County town of Paradise. George B. "Machine-gun" Kelly, a petty bootlegger, had, at the insistence of his wife, gone into big-time crime and had already robbed a hayseed bank in Wilmer, Texas, taking a small amount of cash and machine-gunning a guard to death. Kelly was buried in the Cottondale Cemetery near Paradise, Texas, when he died of a heart attack in Leavenworth prison in 1954, after being returned there from Alcatraz.

This simple concrete marker, almost obscured from view, marks the final resting place of George "Machine-gun" Kelly in the old Cottondale Cemetery in Wise County. The marker seemed incongruous for an outlaw who, at his peak, generated screaming bold headlines. He is buried next to his father-in-law, Robert G. "Boss" Shannon, who was also convicted in the kidnapping of the Oklahoma oilman. (Photo by Bill Binnig)

We found this original "Eighter from Decatur" sign on display at Hollis Jones' Dairy Queen in Decatur. (Photo by Bill Binnig)

"Eighter (or Ada) From Decatur"

While many towns, counties, and regions of Texas offer some historical event or native son as their "claim to fame," not so with Decatur, the county seat of Wise County. Their town, to some residents' chagrin, is remembered for a crapshooter's chant. Few with a penchant for rollin' the bones have not heard a shooter, in a verbal encouragement to the dice to stop on their needed point of eight, sing out, "Eighter (or Ada) from Decatur, county seat of Wise!"

This plaintive chant has made the Texas city known to at least a small group throughout the United States. Military men, especially sailors, who have a reputation for shooting craps, have, during two world wars, widened the scope of the town's fame to include many countries worldwide.

This dubious claim to fame was recognized by the Decatur Chamber of Commerce, which capitalized on the famous chant by installing suitable signs on Highway 287 near the city. The signs, it is believed, were installed between 1938 and 1940. The signs, which pictured a pair of dice showing double fours, included the words, "Sure. . . it's in Texas EIGHTER FROM DECATUR county seat of Wise." Although disdained by some residents as "Not enhancing to Decatur," the signs were repainted when they fell in disrepair.

It is said there was indeed an Ada in Decatur. We were advised that she was a "high stepper" and did frequent Fort Worth, where she became known as "Ada from Decatur." One person informed us that Ada was friendly with the young men and was known to hang around the courthouse square where craps games were frequently played. Sometimes the shooters could be heard saying, "Ada from Decatur!" One of the original signs hangs in Hollis Jones' Dairy Queen in Decatur.

Milford's Honest But Unusual Claim to Fame

Perhaps the most unusual way of remembering a town with little other claim to fame is that employed by the tiny Ellis County town of Milford. If you drive south from

Dallas on Highway 77, you will be welcomed to Milford by their famous—and honest—identification sign. The sign reads, "Welcome to Milford, a city of about 700 friendly people plus 3 or 4 old grouches!"

A representative of the town's Chamber of Commerce advised us, "Although we are quite proud of our town, we are aware of the fact that it is no doubt best known for that sign than any other single thing associated with Milford."

Milford, Texas' claim to fame is its unusual, but honest, welcome signs located at each end of town. (Photo by Marianne Cannon)

Resurrected Namesake and "The Smallest Skyscraper in the World"

Gleaning out Texas locations with unusual claims to fame requires a heap of looking, but in Texas where excess seems to be the norm, we found one Texas city with not one but two (count 'em) genuinely unusual claims to fame. Wichita Falls, we are told by learned historians, "Was named for a five-foot waterfall on the Wichita River," which died of natural causes over a hundred years ago, some say. Texans disdain giving up such icons as a namesake, and civic pride demanded rehabilitation of the falls. In the middle 1980s city fathers decided that just as there was a rock wall in Rockwall, there should be a falls in Wichita Falls.

The original little falls was replaced by a more impressive, if man-made, falls in a park off US 287 near downtown, which was dedicated in 1987. Although in a different location

The city of Wichita Falls once again has a waterfall. Although man-made, the city is rightfully proud of the new falls that replaced the original five-foot fall, which was destroyed by flood. (photo courtesy City of Wichita Falls)

It is easy to see why Wichita Falls' "Littlest skyscraper" stood out among its neighboring buildings before they were torn down. (Photo courtesy Chuck Woodall)

than the original namesake, once again the city has a falls to match its name!

Believe It Or Not

"The world's littlest skyscraper" stands today in this city named for a waterfall. Located at 701 LaSalle is a building shrouded in mystery. The building is a "four-story skyscraper." Each story was only eight by twelve feet, and there were no staircases in the original structure. No means of access to the upper three floors.

The building was built in about 1918. One account, furnished by the Kemp Public Library, says that "An early day promoter sold shares in the building all over the United States, describing the proposed edifice as eighty feet by one hundred twenty feet." The actual dimensions were reduced on the plans to inches, and so the resulting pygmy came into being.

Having no usable space inside, the investors were bilked out of hundreds of thousands of dollars. It is also said that Ripley's Believe-It-or-Not featured it as "The smallest skyscraper in the world." Whatever the accuracy of such accounts, it does stand apart from its neighbors, our information concludes.

Cuero's "Turkey Trot"

Although it may sound like one, this DeWitt County city's unusual claim to fame is no dance, but a parade of sorts. Each year since 1912 turkey buyers have driven a flock of the birds through Cuero to herald the opening of the fall market season. After buying turkeys from outlying farms, buyers drive the gobblers into Cuero. Dubbed "the turkey trot," this ritual underscores this South Texas county's claim to being "the turkey capital of the world."

Paris, Texas' Jesus in Cowboy Boots

One man's religious faith, combined with an unusual sense of humor, has resulted in one of our state's most unusual tourist attractions. This unusual claim to fame is a monument in a cemetery. Both the Paris, Texas Chamber of Commerce and the city's Evergreen Cemetery acknowledge that this marker is one of the city's most visited tourist attractions. Although the city has much more to make it a desirable place to visit, once visitors learn of the unique marker known as "Jesus in cowboy boots," many add this statue to their "things to see" list.

The robe of a cross-bearing Jesus atop Willett Babcock's grave marker is raised enough to reveal the Lord Jesus wearing cowboy boots. The grave marker is so well known it has been placed on Paris' city tours. (Photo by Marianne Cannon)

Representatives at Evergreen Cemetery tell us that Willett Babcock, over whose grave the unusual statue stands, was "the maker of fine furniture." Mr. Babcock built the first opera house in the city of Paris, and he founded the city's fire department, where he served as chief. Mr. Babcock lived and died in the latter part of the nineteenth century. It is said that he envisioned his Lord Jesus as wearing cowboy boots. He instructed a Mr. Klein, a local stone carver, to make an elaborate monument for his final resting place.

The monument was topped with a statue of Jesus wearing cowboy boots. The monument is visited by thousands each year and is so well known, the Paris Chamber of Commerce was prompted to put out a postcard bearing a photo of the unusual marker.

"Uplift City," Texas Town Known for Brassiere Factory

McLean, located 35 miles from Oklahoma in Gray County, was the last Texas town bypassed by Interstate 40, resulting in its losing its spot on the fabled Route 66. But this is not the town's most unusual claim to fame. This town was once known as "Uplift City" because of a brassiere factory built in McLean in the late 1950s. Marie's Foundations was important to the region's economy because of employment opportunities.

The factory building is now occupied by Delbert Drew's Devil's Rope and Route 66 Museum. The barbed wire exhibited there is a far cry from the comfort of the ladies undergarments once turned out there!

The brassiere factory that gave McLean its nickname "Uplift City" is now home of Devil's Rope Museum.

Rattlesnakes and Wasps

Although rattlesnakes and wasps sound more like the residents of an abandoned line shack in the Big Bend country, they are both highly touted by the Sweetwater Chamber of Commerce as valuable attributes of that city, and rightly so!

When one realizes that this friendly but earlier lackluster town started as a store in a dugout on Sweetwater Creek, it is easy to see why the city's world famous "Rattlesnake Roundup," as well as the home base of the heroic Women Air Force Service Pilots of WW II, better known as W.A.S.P.s, are touted as the city's claim to fame.

This western diamondback rattlesnake waits to be weighed in and measured at Sweetwater's annual Rattlesnake Roundup, for which the city is famous.

The "World's Largest Rattlesnake Round-Up," which is forty years old, resulted in 3,942 pounds of western diamondback rattlers being rounded up in 1998, which is below the 40-year average of 5,824 pounds per year. The record length is 81 inches. The Jaycees, who buy the catches, pay from $3.50 to $5.00 per pound, based upon total weight offered. The roundup was held in March 1998. This event, though an unusual claim to fame, has earned bragging rights for this vitally alive Texas city.

Best Little Claim to Fame in Texas

La Grange, county seat of Fayette County, is, without a doubt, most famous for a historic bordello, known throughout Texas as "the Chicken Ranch." The roots of this rural palace of sin can be traced back to 1844. According to published news reports, it operated part of its 130-year tenure with the knowledge and perhaps protection of a local lawman.

Known as a place of initiation into manhood of Texas A&M freshmen, the house of ill repute was operated since 1952 by a madam known to customers as "Miss Edna." Edna Milton came to the ranch from Oklahoma in 1952 at the age of twenty-three. The famous Texas brothel was closed in 1973 as the result of an exposé by well-known Houston TV newsman Marvin Zindler. The attack on the bordello that had become a Texas institution generated so much publicity that it became the inspiration for a movie and a Broadway play entitled *The Best Little Whorehouse in Texas*.

The Infamous Box 13 Political Scandal

The city of Alice in Jim Wells County and neighboring Duval County are unalterably linked to the political scandal that is still examined fifty years later. The year is 1948, and Texan Lyndon B. Johnson is locked in political combat with popular Coke Stevenson for a U.S. Senate seat. Stevenson had apparently won the bitterly fought race until an amended tally from precinct 13 in Jim Wells County gave Johnson enough additional votes to win the election by a margin of 87 votes out of a million votes cast. This squeaker gave Johnson a nickname that would stay with him until he died—"Landslide Lyndon." Johnson was accused of stealing the election with the help of political boss George Parr, known as "The Duke of Duval," who allegedly had the ballot box stuffed in Johnson's favor. This was a giant step in the direction of the White House. Alice and these two counties have a claim to fame that borders on being criminal!

Center Oak

According to *Famous Trees of Texas* published by the Texas Forestry Service, an 1870 geographical survey placed the geographical center of Texas at a spot in Mills County known then as Hughes Store. This community, based upon these findings, changed its name to Center City.

In the town was a large live oak tree, in the shade of which children learned their letters before a schoolhouse was built. Judge J.P. Grundy held court under its branches between 1887 and 1890 while the courthouse was being built in Goldthwaite, the county seat. The tree shaded what amounted to an outdoor post office, as personal mailboxes were placed beneath the tree and residents waited for the mail carrier to deliver the mail. Early stage-coaches met at the tree on their journeys to and from neighboring towns. They off-loaded passengers and freight, as well as changed horses.

The tree was considered by most to be the geographical center of the state. It is easy to see why emotions ran wild

This photo of Center City's historic oak tree in Mills County is courtesy of Glynn Collier, Goldthwaite, Texas.

when locals learned that the tree was scheduled to be destroyed to make way for highway 84. The Highway Department relented. As a result, while most of Center City is no longer standing, the tree is there today, a living marker of the center of Texas!

Regency Suspension Bridge

Without meaning to be unkind, it is accurate, if a bit painful, to say that without their unusual claim to fame, some regions of Texas would have nothing at all, except, perhaps, their personal pride. Such is the case of the Mills County community of Regency. At its peak, so we were told, the community had only a few houses and one store to serve the needs of its residents. And now it has even less. But what it does have is listed on the National Historic Register. That is Regency's unusual claim to fame!

With the vast Colorado River slicing through Mills County and lying between its few residents and the county seat of Goldthwaite, its residents were expected to circum-navigate the river to get into town. In 1903 the area's first bridge across the Colorado was built. This was the first Regency suspension bridge. It served ranchers and farmers to get to market. The bridge fell in 1929 killing a boy, a horse, and some cattle. Its successor was demolished. A contract was made with the Austin Bridge Company of Dallas to build another bridge. The new Regency bridge was erected in 1939. It was a marvelous example of suspension bridges. For that time, one can only imagine the immense pride this almost nonexistent community had with its exemplary suspension bridge!

Although few people reside in today's Regency, the bridge remains as a symbol of rural tenacity and problem

This photo of the Regency "swinging bridge" in Mills County is courtesy of Glynn Collier, Goldthwaite, Texas.

solving. Regency suspension bridge can be seen on County Road 125 off FM 574, 14 miles west of Goldthwaite, Texas. The *Goldthwaite Eagle* newspaper was quick to point out that the bridge could be seen at the beginning of each "Eight Country Reporter" show with Bob Phillips.

The Town Known as a Mailbox

Anyone who was around in the 1940s and '50s, prior to our addiction to that new idea called TV, and who listened to late night radio, will remember those high-wattage, commercial-laden radio stations broadcasting from across the Rio Grande. If you happen to be one of the 500 or so residents of the El Paso County town of Clint, you were certainly aware that your tiny hometown was gaining notoriety across North America as a mailbox for listeners, who ordered any one of the dozens of products offered, to send their money to. The announcers on the Mexican radio stations would advise listeners to send their money to "Clint, that's C-L-I-N-T, Texas!"

Texas' Sweetest Claim to Fame

If not the most unusual claim to fame, surely one of the sweetest claims to fame is that of the Rio Grande Valley's city of Mission. This oasis in the heart of Texas' citrus belt claims to be the capital of the ruby red grapefruit growth in Texas.

The Ezekiel Airship

Although the East Texas town of Pittsburg is known far and wide throughout Texas by sausage aficionados for its extra spicy hot-link sausage, it has, however, another claim to fame that warranted the state of Texas to erect a historical marker in the town. It was in this town that Baptist preacher Burrell Cannon (no relation to the author) built the Ezekiel airship, billed by the Pittsburg Chamber of Commerce as "Man's first powered flight." While this claim might be disputed by some, enough interest was generated in the airplane, actually more of a helicopter, to warrant the historical marker.

The airship was built by the Rev. Cannon in the Pittsburg Machine Shop one year prior to the Wright Brothers' historic flight in 1903 at Kittyhawk. The odd-shaped craft, according to its publicists, "Flew the skies over Pittsburg."

This may be somewhat of an exaggeration. The craft made its first flight in 1902 from a pasture that belonged to the owner of the machine shop where the craft was built. It could be said that the craft was divinely inspired. Rev. Cannon, a life-long student of the Bible, was particularly intrigued by the Bible's account of Ezekiel's vision of God and strange flying creatures that were propelled by wheels. (Ezekiel 1: 16-19).

From such description an idea was born. Rev. Cannon's airship had large, fabric-covered wings. It was propelled by

This stock certificate issued by the Ezekiel Air Ship Manufacturing Company is a sample of those issued to stockholders in Pittsburg, Texas.

an engine that turned four sets of paddles mounted on wheels. Publicity says that those present at the first flight reported that when the engine first started, "The aircraft lurched forward for a short distance, rising vertically into the air. It traveled a few feet and then began to drift for a short distance." The description goes on to say, "The airship was vibrating considerably, so the engine was turned off and it came back to earth." The first flight was hardly flying through the skies over Pittsburg, as was reported.

The airship was being shipped by rail to St. Louis where it was to be exhibited at the World's Fair. A storm, however, blew it off the flatbed car near Texarkana, Texas, and it was destroyed. Legend has it that Rev. Cannon said, "God never willed that the airship would fly, I want no more to do with it!" He left it where it lay.

Cannon had formed the EZEKIEL AIR SHIP MANU-FACTURING COMPANY, and stock in the airship company sold around Pittsburg for $25 per share. A replica, built by the Pittsburg Optimist Club, can be seen at Warwick's Restaurant in Pittsburg.

Longest of the Longhorns

The longest span of horns in the world is said to belong to a Texas steer by the name of Amigo Yates. The steer supporting this record hat rack spends his day under the broiling Texas sun in a pasture outside the tiny town of Tuscola, Texas, just south of Abilene. This survivor of the once-dying breed that developed into a Texas icon is owned by rancher Fayette Yates. The steer's horns measure 103 inches from tip to tip. It was animals such as these that made Texas famous as a beef-producing state.

"Amigo Yates" owned by Fayette Yates of Tuscola, Texas, proudly displays his world record 103-inch horn span. This longhorn would make any town eager to claim him as a famous resident.

Happy Valentine

The town of Valentine (pop. 236) in Jeff Davis County will postmark between 8,000 and 20,000 pieces of mail during the month of February. Due to the high volume of requests for postmarks for St. Valentine's Day, this tiny town will set a record for postal cancellations (all by hand) in February. Only counties of much larger populations will postmark more than the tiny town of Valentine.

The Town Without a Toothache

Another town that fits the profile of having an unusual claim to fame is the Panhandle town of Hereford, county seat of Deaf Smith County. This town was named for the massive herds of Hereford cattle in the region, which were significant enough to bring recognition to the town; however, its name gave way to a hidden asset that more nearly suited a publicist's formula for generating fame. It was discovered that the children of Hereford had fewer cavities and other tooth defects than was known in other Texas regions. This was enough to establish bragging rights in any town. A study revealed that the town's water and soil had an exceptional amount of minerals, including natural fluoride.

This deterrent to tooth decay was a publicist's dream. The town became known as "the town without a toothache." The phenomenon, bolstered by the catchy boast, brought Hereford to the attention of the United States, as well as to the eyes of the world, through the many newspapers and magazines that picked up on the story.

Bowie County's Largest Baby

The following physical description of a famous Texan might not be much of a surprise to those of us who watched him for so many years on TV. He was born in DeKalb, Bowie County, Texas, in 1928. He was reported as the largest baby born in Bowie County, weighing 14 pounds at birth. He was over six feet tall and weighed 200 pounds at age twelve. By the time he became a star football player at Sul Ross University in Alpine, Texas, he was six foot four inches and weighed 275 pounds. This Texas-size Texan was born Bobby Don Blocker but used the Hollywood moniker Dan Blocker when he played "Hoss" Cartwright on NBC's *Bonanza*.

Named by Presidential Order

Burkburnett, fourteen miles north of Wichita Falls in Wichita County, was originally called Nesterville, as it was established by nesters on land that was part of Samuel Burk Burnett's vast Four Sixes ranch. It was later changed to Gilbert. In 1905 President Theodore Roosevelt was Burk Burnett's guest for a wolf hunt at the ranch. He had such a grand time he ordered the U.S. Postal Service to change the name of Gilbert to Burkburnett in honor of his host. The town became the only community in Texas named by order of a president.

Golf Course in the Sky

Marfa, Texas, can claim the highest golf course in Texas. No! Not exorbitant green fees. At over one mile above sea level, this city's municipal golf course is the highest elevation in Texas.

Texas' Smallest State Park

The smallest state park in Texas, at one-tenth acre, is the grave site of Elizabeth Crockett, wife of Alamo hero Davy Crockett. Mrs. Crockett stayed home in Tennessee with her children when Davy came to Texas to fight the Mexicans. Mrs. Crockett came to Texas in 1855 to claim the land granted to Davy for his service at the Alamo. She lived in Hood County until she died there in 1860. Her grave is in Acton, Texas, near Granbury. It is maintained by the Texas Parks and Wildlife Department.

Town Famous for Its Smokestack

The former Erath town of Thurber, located between Mineral Wells and the city of Ranger, has the rare distinction of being known for a red brick chimney. Thurber was established in 1886 as a coal-mining town. When the mine became so unproductive that the coal company couldn't meet its payroll, it was sold to the Texas and Pacific Coal Company and the town was named Thurber.

After the discovery of oil in nearby Ranger, workers in Thurber went on strike for higher wages, influenced by wages paid to oil workers in Ranger. By this time the town, including homes, churches, and schools, had been built for its workers by the coal company and was called Texas and Pacific Coal. The company converted to brick making and moved to Fort Worth.

With no industry the town closed in 1933 and became virtually a ghost town. The last remaining evidence that the town was once a thriving industrial town is a red brick smokestack erected in 1909 as part of the coal company's power plant. A restaurant was built near the relic of a bygone era. A marker at the 128-foot-tall smokestack tells the story of "the most important mine-site in Texas for 30 years." The population sign which once boasted 10,000, now reads pop 5.

The family that owns the Smokestack Restaurant, Randy Bennett, his wife, Andrea, and their three offspring, Robbie, Rusty, and Mollie, are not only its proprietors but

The skyline of the ghost town of Thurber, Texas, pop. 5, is dominated by this smokestack, which was a part of the Texas and Pacific Coal Company that originally owned the town.

are the guardians of the town's few remaining buildings. They comprise the town's total population. The old relic-turned-restaurant can be seen for several miles from several highways.

Post, Texas: Town Made Possible by Breakfast Cereal

C.W. Post first came to Texas in 1895 and lived in Fort Worth. Post suffered from stomach and nervous disorders. In an attempt to get relief he moved to Battle Creek, Michigan, where he entered the Battle Creek Sanitarium. His interest in health caused him to develop a cereal drink, which he named Postum. He also developed breakfast cereals such as Post Toasties and Post Bran. Post was a millionaire many times over when he moved back to Texas in 1906. He purchased a quarter-million-acre ranch in Garza and Lynn Counties on the Texas high plains. At the center of this ranch the businessman founded a town which he called Post City (now Post, Texas, county seat of Garza County).

Post divided the ranch into 160-acre fenced tracts of land with houses on them. Over a twelve-year period, C.W. Post colonized over 1,200 families in the area. Post's health again failed in 1914 and on May 9, 1914, he committed suicide at his home in Santa Barbara, California.

Town's Claim to Fame Yields Clue to Shameful U.S. Indian Policy

If, in your travels through West Texas, you bypassed the business district of the Scurry County seat of Snyder, you missed seeing one of the state's most obviously unusual

Statue of cereal entrepreneur, C.W. Post, founding father of Post, Texas, greets visitors in front of the Garza County courthouse.

claims to fame. On the town square stands a statue of a buffalo. Not just any of the thousands of proud animals that once called the South Plains home, this statue commemorates the shooting of one of a mere handful of white buffaloes known to have been seen in the American West! The animal was killed ten miles northwest of Snyder by one of America's most prolific buffalo hunters, J. Wright Mooar.

Mr. Mooar was born in 1851 in Vermont. As a youth, Mooar had heard about buffalo hunting in Kansas. By the time Mooar was nineteen he had saved enough money to form a party of six men and go to Kansas to hunt buffalo. Buffalo meat was sold to the army to feed troops and to railroad construction crews, but the hides were considered worthless. Mooar shipped some hides to his brother, John, in New York City, and there they found a good market. John joined his brother in Kansas, and they worked together to hunt buffalo and market their hides. Mooar set up the first buffalo hunting camp in the Texas Panhandle in 1871. A story of the famed buffalo hunter says that his most serious problem was the lack of a gun suitable for buffalo hunting. He contacted the Sharpes Rifle Company of Bridgeport Conn., who designed and made a gun for $150. The gun became famous as "the Big 50." Later the Sharpes 44 became the favorite with buffalo hunters.

On October 4, 1876, Mooar and a party of four men set up a hunting camp in Scurry County, about ten miles northwest of Snyder on Deep Creek. After surveying the country one day, Mooar returned to camp about sunset. The sun reflected off a white object in the midst of a buffalo herd. "I quickly saw it was a white buffalo," Mooar said. "Only seven white buffalo were ever seen or killed by white hunters, records show, and I had killed one of them in

Wright Mooar's white buffalo is immortalized in this statue that adorns the Scurry County courthouse square in Snyder, Texas. (Photo courtesy Snyder Chamber of Commerce)

Kansas." Taking another hunter, Dan Dowd, Mooar slipped down Deep Creek toward the herd. Mooar dropped the white buffalo with one shot. He had the buffalo dressed and kept the hide, which was displayed at the St, Louis World's Fair in 1904. The hide was then displayed in the Mooar's home. Experts claim that the odds in the 1800s of an albino calf being born were one in ten million.

By 1877 buffalo hunting had died out, and Scurry County's first settler, J. Wright Mooar, turned to cattle raising.

It was while investigating this event that gives Snyder its unusual claim to fame that we discovered what could be considered by some "another shameful example of the U.S. policy toward the American Indian."

In a conversation with Mrs. Judy Hays, granddaughter of J. Wright Mooar, who owns the hide of Snyder's famous white buffalo, we learned some interesting and disturbing facts about her grandfather's hunting reputation. Mrs. Hays told us that while he did sell buffalo hides, he told her that he hunted buffalo as an agent of the United States government. The American government paid to have the buffaloes slaughtered to get rid of the main food source of the Indians in hopes the Indian problem would dissipate. She said she did not know for whom or what agency her grandfather worked or how he was paid while purging the land of the buffalo. Research shows that U.S. Grant was president while Mr. Mooar was making a name for himself as a buffalo hunter.

Knowing the number of "long knives" that were killed at the hands of the Indians, while making the West safe for settling and in protecting settlers, it is easy to see how the old general, although he might not have authored such a genocidal policy, might readily assent to it.

Red Hot Claim to Fame Linked to East Texas Town

In 1897 Charlie Hasselback of German descent brought the hot link recipe to Camp County. Today they're known as the Pittsburg hot link. The sausage maker was first located in the old Maddox Building, where he sold the links over the counter for preparation at home. Information provided by the Pittsburg Chamber of Commerce advises that "Mr. Hasselback built an addition to the building in 1918 and started serving cooked links over the counter. With wooden counters and benches, the store was less than elaborate. Adding to the simplicity of the hot link business, the links were served with crackers on heavy market paper, and special sauce was provided in soda water bottles. The spicy fare was washed down with cold drinks offered in an assortment of flavors. The links were two for five cents, five for ten cents, and a dozen for a quarter. You could eat them there or carry them out, a custom that became popular with the housewife."

Word about the links spread fast. Pittsburg had two railroad lines, and before long train crews were scheduling their stopovers in Pittsburg, where they could walk up the alley behind the building to eat their noon and evening meals. Truckers and traveling salesmen, hearing of the spicy links, started coming. Folks in nearby towns tried unsuccessfully to match the flavor of the linked sausage in their stores and markets.

So the name Pittsburg Hot Links was originated and continues in use to this day. Mr. Hasselback had two employees. One who bought the livestock, and one who did the butchering. The links were prepared in the market. The thriving business grew yearly. Mr. Hasselback sold the business and additional locations sprung up. A succession of owners resulted in the development of Pittsburg Hot Link Packers, Inc. A far cry from the "five for a dime" business, the company prepares 21,000 to 23,000 pounds of raw hot links per week to be sold in retail stores throughout Texas. Processing their special hot links 40 hours per week, throughout the year, this averages eighteen raw links per minute. Few if any places in Texas can make such a spicy claim to fame!

Glen Rose, Home of Texas' Oldest Unusual Claim to Fame

Glen Rose, county seat of Somervell County, developed around a mill and trading post on the Paluxy River in 1849. Although it was once a health spa, the town enjoys a much older and more durable claim to fame. The first footprints identified as dinosaur tracks were discovered in Wheeler Creek in 1910. Charlie and William Moss found dinosaur tracks in the Paluxy River in 1934. Tracks were chiseled out of the soft limestone and ended up in museums as far away as New York City, as well as in private collections. Preservationists were finally aroused by the loss of the county's natural treasure and the land was eventually incorporated into Dinosaur Valley State Park in 1969. The footprints left by the giant prehistoric lizards that roamed much of Texas qualify as the undisputed oldest claim to fame!

Texas' Battiest Bridge

Most of our places featured as having unusual claims to fame have been cities and towns of Texas. Some were large, while others were mere "wide places in the road." Although not its city's most unusual claim to fame, one of Texas' most visited tourist attractions is a common city bridge in one of our state's major cities. At least it would be common were it not for a natural phenomenon that occurs nightly at the bridge.

The Congress Avenue bridge in Austin is home to an estimated 1.5 million Mexican free-tail bats. About dusk each day visitors to our capital city begin to drift in the direction of the well-publicized bridge. The throng of people gather there to witness the spectacular nightly departure of the bats from their city habitat. A chorus of oohs and aaahs go up from the spectators as a black cyclone-like cloud of bats, wings audibly whirring, wing their way to gorge themselves on the millions of insects that swarm the Colorado River and its environs. This bridge surely holds for its nightly visitors an unusual claim to fame!

Nacogdoches Site of First Christmas in Texas

One of our state's oldest cities is the East Texas city of Nacogdoches. It brags about having its first European settlement in 1716. Age alone has made this historical city a mother lode of Texas trivia. Not only was Nacogdoches the home of some of Texas' most prominent figures, including Sam Houston, Thomas J. Rusk, and Adolphus Stern, the Texas Revolution also was planned in this place.

The city has one claim to fame that is not well known to most Texans. The state's first Christmas celebration was held in Nacogdoches. Although no Sinterklaas, as he was known to the Dutch, who introduced him to America in New York, was present, the holiday was observed. In 1686 the French explorer LaSalle became ill while visiting Nacogdoches. The Tejas Indians nursed him and cured him. Being a devout Catholic, on Christmas Day 1686 LaSalle celebrated a Christmas Mass in Nacogdoches. Information provided us by that city tells us that "no reliable documentation has been found which records an earlier Christmas celebration in Texas." This first Christmas in Texas is colorfully celebrated by that city each year.

Lovable American Trademark Brings Fame to North Texas Town

The innocuous North Texas town of Krum (pronounced crumb by the locals) recently received 24 column inches, including a color photo, on the front page of one section of the *Dallas Morning News*. This is, indeed, a remarkable amount of coverage for this small Denton County community. We say this meaning no offense to the proud people of this hamlet named, according to the *Handbook of Texas*, for the engineer who piloted the first train through there in 1886.

The town that was once a grain center has little to crow about except its beautiful rolling pastureland. It received its enviable publicity because of one of its residents who enjoys celebrity status. This resident is not your run-of-the-mill rural citizen who made good. She is no ingenue in the world of marketing. She is well known and beloved not only in the hearts of Texans, but Americans everywhere. Famous for her big brown eyes and loving behavior, the popularity of this Krum resident started in 1938 when her likeness with the well-known garland of daises encircling her neck helped promote Borden milk products. Yes! We are speaking of Elsie, the Borden cow.

As a child I remember my parents taking me to see her and Elmer when they bedded down in their bovine boudoir in the Old Mill at the annual State Fair of Texas. To see a nationally known trademark in person was a thrill to a school-aged boy with my curiosity. Although this Elsie is the twenty-ninth in a long line of cows selected to represent the Borden Company's products, she is certainly an unusual claim to fame for this Denton County town. Elsie is, according to John Marchman, owner of Marchman and Associates of Denton, the advertising agency hired to book the numerous tours and personal appearances of the lovable logo, "probably the most spoiled cow on earth."

The gentle folks of Krum can be proud of the fame this American advertising icon has brought to their docile community. Krum's Elsie, like many other famous Texans, was born elsewhere. The native of Ohio moved to Texas a year ago when a Dallas businessman bought nine Borden dairies in Texas, Louisiana, and Mississippi. The deal included the Borden name, logo, and the real-life Elsie.

Henderson's Historical Outhouse

If you are fortunate enough to visit the beautiful and industrious East Texas city of Henderson, county seat of Rusk County, query its locals as to "What is Henderson's claim to fame?" The answers you get will vary depending on the time of year and whom you ask.

If you are one of the thousands who flock there in November for the town's annual syrup festival, you will most certainly be told that this town, named for a man who was destined to become Texas' first governor, is "famous for its ribbon cane syrup." This is easy to accept as fact when

Built for Henderson lawyer John Arnold and his family from plans ordered from Sears Roebuck and Company, Henderson's famous three-holer is said to be the only outhouse in Texas, and maybe the nation, to achieve historical status. It is certainly Texas' most publicized historical marker. (Photo courtesy Henderson's Depot Museum)

one sees that all the visitors, upon leaving town, are carrying a shiny tin gallon bucket of the just-cooked, ready-for-soppin' East Texas cane syrup!

On the other hand, you might be told that Henderson is the site of the Daisy Bradford No. 3 oil well, which wildcatter C.M. "Dad" Joiner drilled and which was the gusher that brought in the "richer-beyond-all-imagination" East Texas oil field.

But regardless of whom you ask, if you modify your question to "What is Henderson's most unusual claim to fame?" the answer will unanimously be "Arnold's historical outhouse." After you close your gaping mouth, you will find that you can see the notorious privy at the city's Depot Museum. It is the only structure of that type to be awarded historical status in Texas, maybe in the nation. A helpful representative of the Henderson Chamber of Commerce advised us that when the application for a historical marker for the outhouse was submitted, they were asked if the letters c and r had inadvertently been omitted from courthouse. It seemed that no one had ever requested historical recognition of an outhouse, thus the assumption that a typographical error resulted in "outhouse."

The privy which, in most cases, would be the butt (pardon the pun) of giggle-provoking jokes is not one to be snickered at! This elaborate three-holer was built in 1908 for Henderson lawyer John R. Arnold and his family. It features double-walled construction for insulation in both summer and winter. Windows were added to facilitate reading. The Sears and Roebuck catalog is not in the privy for that pastime. The business end of the outhouse, located along the back wall, has three holes to accommodate deferent sizes. The holes are tastefully outfitted with wooden lids with ceramic handles, a feature not common in rural outhouses.

German Town's Claim to Fame is "Coffee Mill"

It seems highly out of character that Texas, with its reputation for pomposity, would have a town whose claim to fame was something as mundane as a coffee mill. Try telling that to the proud German folks in the Hill Country town of Fredericksburg! In 1846 German settlers immigrating to Texas were sponsored by a German organization known as the Adelsverein, or Association of Noblemen.

One of the town's first buildings was its Vereins Kirche, or Associations church. Built in 1847, the structure was to serve not only as a church, but also as a meeting hall, library, and fort. These amenities had been promised the Germans by the Verein. The one multipurpose building allowed the sponsors to keep their promise. The octagonal shaped building was, for obvious reasons, dubbed "the coffee mill." The original structure was torn down in 1897. A replica was built in 1934-35. The building now houses a photographic history of the early settlers.

Fredericksburg's 152-year-old Vereins Kirche, known locally as "The Coffee Mill" because of its shape, now houses a photographic history of the town's early settlers. Its octagonal shape is unique in the Texas Hill Country. (Photo by Gerti Darius).

Part II

Minor Luminaries

*W*hen at the end of a stage play the actors come out for their curtain calls, it is easy to single out the main characters for applause. It is the cast of supporting characters who wait till last to take their bows, even though some of these "minor luminaries" gave us some of our most memorable moments during the performance. Such is the case in the development of Texas. The cast of leading notables who made Texas great are known by name by nearly every school-age Texas child. It has been some of the minor luminaries of both the nineteenth and twentieth centuries who have given Texas some of its brightest moments!

Some of them have only been character actors on Texas' stage of life, but what memories they have left for us. We have reserved this section of our trivia book for a few of them to take their bows. Our stage would be far too crowded if we presented all the minor luminaries who have earned recognition. The few offered here will give an idea of the type of supporting actors who have built on the foundation of our Texas heroes!

Frank Hamer, Nemesis of the Barrow Gang

The man who wrote *finis* to the exploits of the infamous team of Clyde Barrow and his youthful moll Bonnie Parker was Texas Ranger captain Francis Augustus Hamer, better known as Frank or Pancho.

Hamer enlisted in the Rangers in 1906. He resigned from the Rangers several times only to return to fight Texas crime. In 1932 Hamer retired from active duty but retained his commission. In 1934 he was recalled by Governor Miriam (Ma) Ferguson to track down the infamous bandit team of Clyde Barrow and Bonnie Parker, who had made themselves a national legend and folk heroes to many who thought them champions of the poor.

After a three-month search, Hamer, with the assistance of other lawmen, trapped the pair, whose name struck terror in the hearts of bankers and lawmen alike, near Gibsland, Louisiana. They were shot and killed in a Hamer-engineered ambush!

Pompeo Coppini, Italian-Born Texas Treasure

Maxine Mayes' "Coppini's Passion," appearing in the *Texas Highways* January 1999 issue, artfully introduced to us a minor luminary known up to now more by his powerful works than by his name. Born in northern Italy in 1870,

Pompeo Coppini, whose parents had planned for him to be a civil engineer, was destined for greatness in a far more creative field and in a then far remote corner of the world. Ms. Mayes artistically unfolds the story of how Coppini, like another esteemed Texas sculptor, Elizabeth Ney, had to challenge parental expectations to pursue his artistic talent. And are we glad he did!

As Ms. Mayes put it, "Monuments across Texas bear silent witness to his passion for art and the pride he took in his adopted state." At age thirty-one the Italian-born sculptor arrived in Texas after first studying at the Academy of Fine Arts in Florence and in 1896 immigrating to the United States, where he got a toe-hold on his new country, living in New York City. Ms. Mayes tells us that this talented artist unloaded lumber on a Hudson River pier for seventy-five cents a day.

The artisan who created the much admired and photographed cenotaph that stands in front of the Alamo, arrived in Texas in 1901. He came at the request of a San Antonio stone dealer who had a contract to erect a Confederate memorial in Austin. The stone dealer had selected Coppini to sculpt a statue of Jefferson Davis. Fate had dealt Texas a winning hand. Coppini and Texas became fast friends. Although warned against coming to Texas by a friend who declared Texas "a wild state where they are shooting at each other," Coppini saw in Texas "The real America I had been dreaming of."

Although Coppini's trail through Texas is lined with numerous famous monuments, it piques our personal interest with a detour through Dallas in a most poignant turn. While working on a monument for Francis Scott Key before coming to Texas, the Italian immigrant needed a model for a figure to be carved at the base of the monument. Ms. Mayes writes, "He found the perfect model in Elizabeth (Lizzie) Barbieri of New Haven, Connecticut. As Lizzie worked for the sculptor, his admiration and love for her grew. They were married on February 27, 1898." The Coppinis remained childless, except for a foster daughter, Waldine Tauch, a talented young sculptor who became Coppini's protégée. And "Here," as someone said, "is the rest of the story."

In this same chapter we present William J. McDonald, the Texas Ranger who is credited with creating the Ranger motto "One Riot—One Ranger." The bronze statue of the Texas Ranger, entitled "One Riot—One Ranger," that stands in the terminal of Dallas Love Field airport was sculpted by Waldine Amanda Tauch, the foster child of Pompeo Coppini. We highly recommend reading the full story of Coppini by Maxine Mayes. We are grateful to Ms. Mayes for permission to use excerpts from her story to create this cameo of Coppini in our book.

Harriet Potter, Bell Weather for Common-Law Marriage Recognition

A Texas granite marker partially funded by a local funeral home is, at least for now, the only marker recognizing the Texas pioneer woman who may well have set the standard by which common-law marriages became accepted in Texas. The simple marker bearing the inscription "To honor and remember Harriet Potter Ames bravest woman in Texas" stands on a little plot of East Texas soil near her Caddo Lake home. If the members of the Caddo Lake Historical Research Committee have their way, the stone soon will be augmented by a Texas historical marker, which the committee says is long overdue!

Recently dedicated marker honoring the memory of Harriet Potter, erected near the Potter home at Caddo Lake. (Photo courtesy Marcia Thomas)

Although her burial place is not known, this woman has earned a place in the pages of Texas history. Much of what is known of this pioneer Texas woman is found in her auto-biography, written during the final days of her life at age eighty-three while she was living with her daughter in New Orleans. What is known is that she lived in Texas during some of its most tumultuous years! Marcia Thomas, one of her boosters on the committee, calls her "the epitome of the pioneer woman."

Born in New York in 1810, Harriet Ann Moore's life runs parallel to the birth of Texas. Harriet married Solomon Page, who fought in the Texas War of Independence. Page stranded his wife and two children on the South Texas prai-rie, where she found herself caught up in the famous "Runaway Scrape," the hysterical flight of Texas residents fleeing their homes ahead of what they thought was Santa Anna's Army. Harriet, thinking her husband had been killed in the Battle of San Jacinto, took up with her rescuer, Robert Potter, a signer of the Texas Declaration of Independence, and for whom Potter County was to be named.

In her memoirs Harriet said her marriage to Potter had been by bond. "An agreement signed before witnesses." The freedom fighter and his wife lived together for seven years. They considered their marriage acceptable as common-law marriage. They moved to land Potter had been granted for his military service. The property on Caddo Lake was called "Potter's Point."

In 1842 Potter was rousted out of bed and shot in the head while trying to escape enemies he had made while involved in the East Texas "Regulator-Moderator War." This was a little-known rebellion against the Republic of Texas. Following Robert's cruel death, Harriet tried to inherit Potter's land. She was unable to do so because it was held that she and Potter were not legally married. Harriet Potter's fruitless court battle to prove herself Potter's legal wife was the foundation for today's laws that recognize common-law marriage, according to historians.

Ms. Thomas' play *Texian Woman* was presented as a benefit to raise funds to buy the property on which the marker stands. Ms. Thomas presents her original play, which has received rave reviews, regularly at the Living Room Theater (903) 665-2310.

Howard Hughes

One time-worn bromide advises, "Power corrupts; absolute power corrupts absolutely!" Some would argue that the same could be said for money! Anyone so postulating might hold up as proof of their theory a well-known Texan of the twentieth century, Howard Hughes, son of Howard R. Hughes of Houston's famed Hughes Tool Company. As scion of the wealthy Hughes fortune, young Howard used his inherited fortune in what appears to be a self-serving fashion.

He did have some accomplishments of his own of which he could be justly proud. He started flying at age fourteen, and the millionaire became an accomplished aviator, having set the world land speed record for a plane (352 mph) in 1935. In 1937 he set a new transcontinental speed record (7 hours 28 minutes), and in 1938 he established a new round-the-world record (91 hours 14 minutes). In 1941 Hughes designed, built, and flew (one time) what was then the world's largest plane, known as the "Spruce Goose" because of its plywood construction. The behemoth had a wingspan of 320 feet.

Hughes evidently didn't find his aviation prowess ful-filling enough, as he later directed his attention to making motion pictures. He started in his usual Hughes modest way by purchasing the well-known RKO movie studios. Howard Hughes then proceeded to sign some of Holly-wood's most luscious and voluptuous starlets, filling their pretty heads with his dreams of making them stars.

One of Hughes' big discoveries was beautiful, full-figured brunette Jane Russell. He selected this head-turner to star in a Western he was to make in 1940, *The Outlaw*. The film was to be Hughes' most famous. It starred Miss Russell and created a sensational uproar with her "romp-in-the-hay" scene. The posters and stills offered to promote the film were frowned upon by many theaters as "too risqué to post below theater marquees." As promised, the film did launch Jane Russell into her film career.

Along with his success in making motion pictures came certain eccentricities. The rich Texan developed a driving phobia about germs and disease. His phobia manifested itself by his washing and bathing several times a day. This escalated into his attempt at total isolation from germs. He disinfected his telephone constantly. Hughes did not allow even his closest associates and longtime business confi-dants to approach him. He touched practically no one. His eating habits were so unorthodox he was subject to ill-nesses, which he blamed on everything but his own eccentricities.

In his twilight years he moved, along with his meticu-lously selected staff (most of whom were of the Mormon faith, which he thought more trustworthy), to a Las Vegas hotel where he and his entourage occupied several floors. While there the once handsome young man with the Clark Gable mustache began to permit his personal appearance to deteriorate, letting his fingernails and toenails grow to an abnormal length. His unbarbered hair grew long and matted, as did his beard. His phobias, agitated further by numerous legal entanglements, drove the multimillionaire to become a total recluse. Contemporary photos reveal him as looking the part of a cave-dwelling hermit!

As his bizarre life drew near an end, Howard Hughes started living in hotels outside the U.S.A. The heir to the Hughes Tool Company, whose holdings once included the RKO motion picture studios and Trans World Airlines, died a recluse, among rumors and ridicule, on an airplane bringing the ailing millionaire from Acapulco, Mexico, to a hospital in Houston, on April 5, 1976.

Bonham's "Mr. Speaker" Sam Rayburn

To refer to Samuel Taliaferro Rayburn as a "minor luminary" is a little akin to calling Texas "big." Both are vastly understated! Sam Rayburn was Speaker of the House of Representatives longer than any other man. This man who was the epitome of a politician was born in 1882, the son of a Confederate soldier who refused to accept a commission because of his embarrassment over his inability to read or write. Rayburn moved to Texas when he was five years old. He attended country schools and developed an interest in politics. On the brink of a new century, Texas' first native-born governor, Jim Hogg, was in office.

Rayburn attended Mayo Normal School, now East Texas University in Commerce. He worked at three jobs to support himself. He passed a teachers' examination and taught in Hopkins County for a year before returning to Commerce to finish getting a degree, which was conferred

The dedication of the Rayburn Library in Bonham Oct. 9, 1957, drew an impressive array of politicos. They came to honor the Texan who was Speaker of the House longer than anyone in American history. Shown here are President Lyndon B. Johnson and Ladybird, President Harry S. Truman and Bess, and Sam Rayburn. (Photo courtesy Sam Rayburn Library)

upon him in 1903. Rayburn, the son of an illiterate soldier, won a seat in the House in 1907. He admittedly was afraid of town folks in store-bought clothes.

Prior to election to the Legislature, Sam Rayburn had never been a hundred miles from home. In 1911, at age twenty-nine, Rayburn became the youngest Speaker of the Texas House. When the Congressman from Bonham decided to run for the U.S. Senate, Rayburn announced for Congress. He was elected after a difficult campaign. One of his mentors in Congress was Congressman—later vice president under Franklin Roosevelt—John Nance Garner of Uvalde, Texas.

Following the death of Speaker William Bankhead in 1940, Rayburn became the 92nd Speaker. It was Rayburn who in 1945, when he became aware that Roosevelt was near death, told friends, "I'll have to speak with Harry (Truman) tomorrow. He has to be prepared to carry on a tremendous burden." Truman was in Rayburn's office on April 12, when White House aides located him to inform him of the president's death.

On January 31, 1951, Rayburn exceeded 3,000 days as Speaker of the House. Rayburn was once quoted as saying, in regards to his ascension to power, "I missed being a tenant farmer by a gnat's heel."

Willy Shoemaker

One of horse racing's best-known and winningest jockeys, Willy Shoemaker was born in the El Paso County border town of Fabens.

Julius C. (Jules) Bledsoe, First to Sing "Old Man River"

Jules Bledsoe, a Negro baritone born in Waco, Texas, studied at Bishop College in Marshall, Texas, before entering Columbia University. His diverse voice studies prepared him for his concert debut in the 1927 production of *Showboat* in New York City, where he was the first to sing one of the show's signature songs, "Old Man River."

Elisabet Ney, Eccentric Artist

One of Texas' best-known artists, known for her masterful capturing of Texas heroes in stone, was also known for her eccentricities. Her marble statues of Stephen F. Austin and Sam Houston have an honored place in the Texas State Capitol; duplicates were placed in Statuary Hall in the U.S. Capitol. The German-born sculptress turned Texans on their ear when she retained her maiden name after she married Dr. Edmund Montgomery. She also was given to wearing bloomer-type slacks.

The Montgomerys purchased the limestone plantation house Liendo in Hempstead. It was in this house that the Montgomery's two-year-old child died of diptheria and his remains were cremated in the family's fireplace.

Bill Pickett's Bulldog Grip

Bill Pickett, inventor of steer wrestling, or "bulldogging," was born in Liberty Hill, Texas, of Negro and Choctaw Indian blood. He was a range rider and did odd jobs on various ranches. Once while loading cattle into a stock car he was confronted by a runaway steer. He took the steer by the horns, twisted its neck, and bit into its lip, holding on like a bulldog until the steer fell to the ground. He developed this technique into an act, and in Fort Worth in the 1900s he joined the Miller Brother's Wild West show. The act was so effective that he was credited with inventing the art of steer wrestling, or "bulldogging" as it was known. Pickett's favorite horse bore the unusual name of Spradley.

Texan on Baseball Card

Rogers Hornsby, born April 27, 1896, in Winters, Texas, was called "the greatest right-handed hitter in professional baseball" and was one of the most controversial characters in the game. Although he did not smoke or drink or otherwise dissipate, he was a compulsive horse player whose gambling caused run-ins with managers. He died January 16, 1963, in Chicago and was buried in the family cemetery in Hornsby Bend, Texas, a few miles east of Austin. Commenting on his burial in Central Texas, one eastern writer remarked on the irony of Hornsby being buried 700 miles from the nearest racetrack.

Texas' First Radio Broadcaster

Although his name is not a household word, as are many in the world of entertainment, Leroy Brown holds a special place in the annals of Texas radio broadcasting. Brown was, in all probability, the first radio broadcaster in Texas.

Professor Brown built, as a part of his experiment in high-frequency radio, a transmitter in his physics laboratory on the campus of the University of Texas.

Brown began broadcasting weather and crop reports before WW I. He used the call letters KUT. By March 1922 the station had combined with a second campus station, call letters 5XY, and with a 500-watt power rating was one of the best equipped and one of the most powerful stations in the nation. The station became what is now station KNOW in Austin.

Schuyler B. Marshall Stopped Dallas' Last Lynching

Dallas' last lynching attempt occurred on April 6, 1925. On that date, Schuyler Marshall, sheriff of Dallas County, confronted a mob that attempted to rush the Dallas County jail demanding two convicted rapists be turned over to them for punishment. Two days after Marshall thwarted the mob action, he transported the two men to Huntsville, where they were executed in accordance with the ruling of the court.

Aunt Jemima Was a Texan

The Hearne, Texas, Chamber of Commerce touts one of their own as the model for one of America's best-known trademarks. The Robertson County woman's name was Rosie Lee Moore. Her story includes the history of the face that has looked down on millions of kitchens from the boxes of Aunt Jemima pancake flour and bottles of corresponding syrup. The black woman who represented Quaker Oats Company as Aunt Jemima from 1950 until her death in 1967 is buried in the Central Texas county's Hammond Colony cemetery, less than a dozen miles from Hearne.

The legend of Aunt Jemima, according to the information provided by the Chamber, tells us that Aunt Jemima began in fact prior to the Civil War in rural Louisiana. She was a cook on a plantation owned by Col. Higbee and was well loved for her pancakes. After the war a northern flour mill bought the rights to make a ready-made mix of pancake flour. Aunt Jemima went along to promote this new flour.

Over the years following, several women played the part of Aunt Jemima for Quaker Oats Company. The last real

Aunt Jemima, however, was our Texas connection. After a failed marriage, Rosie Lee Moore moved to Oklahoma and remarried. Rosie took a job with Quaker Oats Company and while working in the advertising department was "discovered" and took over the role of Aunt Jemima. The Texas Aunt Jemima toured the country for Quaker Oats, returning to Hearne at Christmastime, until her death in 1967.

Minor Luminaries with a Spanish Flavor

Although the roles they played in the development of Texas from a part of Mexico to an independent republic and helping it progress into a state has not made their names as indelibly etched in our minds as other Texans of the time, our Tejano heroes, in their own right, deserve much credit in building the Texas of today!

"Tejanos" were Texans of Mexican heritage living in early day Texas. Among the first Tejanos to come to the fore for Texas was **Gregorio Esparza**. Although his brother, Francisco, was fighting for General Santa Anna against the Texians at the Alamo, this Tejano elected to fight for Texas independence at the Alamo. When the Mexican general gave orders for his soldiers to gather the bodies of the slain Alamo defenders to be burned, Francisco Esparza began searching for the body of his brother, Gregorio. When he found the slain Tejano, he and his widowed sister-in-law went to Santa Anna to beg for the body so they could give it a Christian burial. Santa Anna relented and let them remove Gregorio's body. He was buried near the San Fernando church, the only defender accorded such an honor.

Lorenzo De Zavala Although a Mexican by birth and a former holder of numerous appointed and elected positions in Mexico, the educated De Zavala, who was an ardent liberal, was granted an impresario's contract to introduce 500 families into Texas. He became an active participant in the Texian's fight for independence because of the injustices shown toward the colonists in Texas by the Mexican government. He was a signer of the Texas Declaration of Independence, and in March of 1836 he was elected vice president of the Republic of Texas. Following the Battle of San Jacinto, which took place near his Buffalo Bayou home, he turned his home into a hospital for wounded Texians and later for wounded Mexicans.

It is a little underrated to call De Zavala a minor luminary in Texas history. We do so because his deeds are not as well known as other principals in our past. This man was a real Tejano hero!

Juan Seguin Born in San Antonio, Seguin was one of the earliest supporters of the Anglo's cause against the Mexican government. Seguin was with James Bowie at the Battle of Concepcion. Seguin escaped the fate of the Alamo defenders because he had been sent through the Mexican lines with a plea for reinforcements. It is Juan Seguin who is given historical credit for giving a military burial to the ashes of the men killed at the Alamo!

Moses Rose (The Alamo Defender Who Saved His Own Hide)

Most every Texas school child has heard the story of Col. Travis drawing a line with his sword in the Alamo dirt before it was soaked with the blood of the defenders of

Texas liberty. According to the legend, he then advised the defenders of the Alamo of the hopelessness of their efforts and solemnly advised them that their struggle was a suicide mission. He also invited those wishing to stay with him to fight for Texas to step across the line and join him. He then told them that anyone wishing to leave the old shrine could do so with a clear conscience and unblemished name. As most of us were taught, only one man elected to take up the commander's offer to save his own hide. Few recall the name of that lone defender who left the Alamo when faced with a suicide mission. Moses Rose is the only Alamo defender whose name is not engraved on the cenotaph that stands in front of this shrine of Texas liberty!

Moses Rose, whose name is actually Louis Rose, was born in France in about 1785. He served in Napoleon's army during the invasion of Russia and Italy. It has been reported that his excuse for leaving the Alamo was "I have been through enough war in my lifetime."

Rose came to Texas in 1826 and had worked in sawmills and as a teamster. He came to San Antonio in 1835 when it was under siege by the Mexicans. He remained with Col. Travis in the Alamo until March 3, 1836. Rose was a swarthy man with black hair and spoke Spanish more fluently than English, which made it possible for him to elude the Mexicans. He stopped in several Texas towns and finally settled in Nacogdoches, where he ran a butcher shop until late 1842. He died near Logansport, Louisiana, about 1850.

Capt. Manuel T. "Lone Wolf" Gonzaullas, Twentieth-Century Texas Ranger

The cessation of hostilities between the Indians of Texas and the white settlers, and the demise of such Old West outlawry as cattle rustling and stagecoach robbery, did not mean there was no longer a need for the legendary Texas Rangers. As the state of Texas developed and was ushered into the modernism of the twentieth century, so did its criminal element make advances. History shows that the talents and bravery of this early law enforcement agency were needed all the more! The mission of the Texas Rangers, who had exchanged their favorite mounts for automobiles and sometimes airplanes, required men with the ability to adjust to the new ways to deal with the new problems spawned by this era of industry and commerce in Texas, while still retaining the intestinal fortitude and tenacity exacted of the early Rangers. Just such a man was M.T. Gonzaullas, better known as "Lone Wolf."

An example of this man's bringing the spirit of the early Texas Rangers into the new era occurred in 1931 when the East Texas oil field blew in. East Texas towns like Kilgore were suddenly overflowing with people from all walks of life hoping to get a piece of the sudden bonanza pie! And among the influx of wealth-seekers, as was to be expected, were the grifters, gamblers, prostitutes, and thugs, whose eyes were focused not on the future of this new era, but on the quick, if illegal, bucks that could be made during such uncontrollable times. Things were so out of control at one point that Governor Ross Sterling declared martial law and sent in the National Guard and the Texas Rangers.

One of the "today" Rangers was then Sgt. Manuel T. Gonzaullas. The Ranger always wore boots and a Stetson hat and carried two revolvers. His very appearance, no doubt, struck terror in the hearts of would-be evildoers, who grew up on the intrigue and mystique of the Texas Rangers. It is said, and on good authority, that men sometimes confessed when told they were about to be questioned by a Ranger. Historians, writing about the crime-laden oil field boomtowns such as in the East Texas field, reported that "Lone Wolf" Gonzaullas prowled the streets forcing idlers to turn up their palms. Those with callused hands were free, and those with smooth hands were gamblers and thugs. He used to shackle them to heavy log chains he called a "trotline." "Lone Wolf" used fishing terminology for his "daily catch."

W.A.A. (Bigfoot) Wallace, Texas Ranger and Teller of Tall Tales

In writing about this colorful figure in Texas history, I rely heavily on the Texas State Historical Association's *Handbook of Texas.*

William Alexander Anderson Wallace was born in Virginia in 1817. It is said that as a Scotsman, his klan was strong in him. We owe his family ties for his being a minor but colorful part of our Texas heritage. When he learned that a brother and a cousin had been shot down in the Goliad Massacre, he set out for Texas, "To take pay out of the Mexicans." He later said that the account had been squared.

Wallace stood six feet two inches in his moccasins and weighed 240 pounds. His size, no doubt, accounted for his descriptive nickname. Wallace quit farming in La Grange in 1840 and moved to Austin. He claimed to have seen the last buffalo in the region run down Congress Avenue. When Wallace decided there were too many people in Austin he moved to San Antonio.

"Bigfoot" volunteered for the ill-fated Mier Expedition, which landed him in the notorious Perote Prison in the Mexican state of Vera Cruz. Following his release from Perote he joined John Coffee (Jack) Hays' company of the Texas Rangers. He served with the Rangers in the Mexican War. In the 1850s, as a captain, he commanded a Ranger company of his own, fighting border bandits as well as Indians.

Wallace drove a mail hack from San Antonio to El Paso. On one occasion, after losing his mules to Indians, he walked to El Paso, and it is said he ate twenty-seven eggs at the first house he came to before continuing on into town for a full meal. The last years of his life were spent in Frio County near a small village named Bigfoot. It is said that Wallace was an avid storyteller with a tendency to "stretch the blanket" or embroider the details.

Samuel Walker, Revolver Designer

In the early days of the settling of Texas, the hand weapon of choice for the settler facing a myriad of threats on the new frontier was the famous knife that bore the name of Alamo hero James Bowie. This was to change in 1831 when Samuel Colt invented his Colt revolver. Patented in February of 1836, the first revolver manufactured was a .34 caliber with a four-and-a-half-inch octagon barrel.

Sometime after the Texas Revolution the Texas Rangers began using the revolvers. One of the Rangers was Maryland-born Samuel H. Walker, who had distinguished himself as an Indian fighter in Georgia and Florida. After coming to Texas he joined Captain John C. Hays' Ranger company. Walker was sent to New York to deal with Samuel Colt regarding the purchase of arms for the Republic of Texas.

When he found Colt he suggested certain modifications to the then popular "Texas revolver." He was responsible for the modified pistol known thereafter as the Walker Colt revolver. This pistol became the weapon of choice for the men of the Texas frontier.

Ranger William J. McDonald, "One Riot—One Ranger"

Ranking along with "Remember the Alamo," and "Come and take it" of Gonzalez fame is the Texas Ranger motto "One riot—One Ranger." This appropriate motto for the state's oldest law enforcement agency is credited to Ranger captain William J. (Captain Bill) McDonald. Stu Lauterbach at the Ranger Museum, quoting

This bronze statue of a Texas Ranger by Waldine Amanda Tauch, bearing the title "Texas Ranger of 1960 One Riot—One Ranger" was given to the City of Dallas by Mr. and Mrs. Earle Wyatt. It stands in the terminal of Dallas' Love Field airport. It was dedicated April 30, 1961, and reinstalled at Love Field Aug. 20, 1984. (Photo courtesy Office of Cultural Affairs City of Dallas)

from McDonald's biography, tells us that McDonald arrived in Dallas alone to halt an illegal boxing match that threatened to turn into a riot. When he stepped off the train, a very nervous Dallas mayor asked, "Where are the rest of the men?" To this, McDonald is supposed to have replied, "Hell, ain't I enough? There ain't but one riot." This motto is graphically perpetuated by a bronze statue of a Texas Ranger that greets travelers in the terminal building of Dallas Love Field airport. Its caption reads "Texas Ranger of 1960 One Riot—One Ranger."

Also credited to the glib and fearless McDonald is a philosophy he verbalized to encourage the men of his company stationed in Amarillo at the turn of the century. He is known for saying, "No man in the wrong can stand up against a fellow that's in the right and keeps on a comin'!" This Ranger died in 1918.

John William Heisman

Football and Texas, especially college football, seem to be inexorably linked. As more and more Texans made their way into college, the competitive spirit was kindled and the football field proved to be the dueling ground where differences were settled. With the advent of professional football and with hometowns and regions having their own franchises, partisanship was destined to flourish. Perhaps to the surprise of some, professional football, whatever the franchise, has an important link to Texas.

The most sought-after players by franchises are those college players who have won the coveted Heisman trophy. This award was named for legendary football coach John William Heisman, who was the first full-time football coach and athletic director at Rice University in Houston, Texas (1924-1927).

John Nance (Cactus Jack) Garner

It is not just "Texas bragging" to say that it seems like some of Texas' so-called "minor luminaries" shine brighter than the major stars of most other states. One example of our state's stellar performers was the thirty-second vice president of the United States, John Nance (Cactus Jack) Garner.

This product of a Red River County, Texas log cabin was the oldest of thirteen children. He earned pocket money playing shortstop for the semipro Coon Soup Hollow Blossom Prairie baseball team. As a lifetime devoteé of baseball, Garner was a familiar figure at baseball games in Washington.

The colorful Texas epitome of a politician didn't start at the top of the political ladder. After spending a semester at Vanderbilt, Garner developed tuberculosis and returned to a dryer Texas climate, where he read law with a law firm. In his first venture into politics he was defeated in his bid for the office of city attorney. It was shortly thereafter that he moved to the South Texas town of Uvalde. While a partner in a law firm he was appointed to fill a vacancy as county judge. He later won an elected term in his office. Garner was elected to the state legislature in 1898. It was as a state legislator that he gained his lifelong nickname "Cactus Jack." His love for the prickly pear caused him to introduce the bloom of this prolific cactus as the state flower of Texas. It lost to the bluebonnet!

It was also as a state legislator that he launched his long-lasting national political career. He won approval of a

John Nance (Cactus Jack) Garner of Uvalde, 32nd Vice President of the United States, suffered one of his most painful political defeats at the hands of Texas women. The Texas branch of the Colonial Dames of America were successful in getting Texas Legislators to vote the blue-bonnet the state flower of Texas instead of Garner's beloved cactus flower, which he proposed for this honor. (Photo courtesy Ettie Garner Memorial Museum)

plan to redistrict a part of South Texas. Not unexpectedly, he ran for and was elected to represent the newly created district in the United States Congress. John Nance (Cactus Jack) Garner was thirty-five years old when he went to Washington as Democratic Representative of the Fifteenth Texas Congressional District. Theodore Roosevelt was president.

By the time World War I came upon us Garner was recognized as the leading Democrat. Although he was considered an isolationist, he voted to declare war on Germany. In Garner's twenty-eighth year in politics he was elected to the high position of Speaker of the U.S. House of Representatives. He was also mentioned as a possible candidate for the presidency. History tells us that Franklin Roosevelt won the nomination with Garner selected as his vice presidential running mate. Roosevelt's success in politics is legendary, and although Garner disapproved Roosevelt's seeking a third term, he remained a staunch Democrat.

He returned to Uvalde after thirty-eight years in the nation's capital. This bright Texas star was the first Texan to be elected to Speaker of the House and the first Texan elected vice president. "Cactus Jack" Garner remained a political voice and lived to endorse John F. Kennedy in 1960 and fellow Texan Lyndon Baines Johnson in 1964. The "Sage of Uvalde" died in 1967 just days shy of his ninety-ninth birthday.

John King Fisher (Flamboyant Gunfighter)

He was described as wearing an ornamented Mexican sombrero, a black Mexican jacket embroidered with gold, a crimson sash and boots, and tiger skin chaps, which seemed hardly the costume of a feared Texas gunslinger. This man of violence was a native of Kentucky. Following the death of his father, he cut his teeth on violence when he was employed by a justice of the peace to discourage rustling activities. The man wore a brace of silver-plated ivory handled revolvers.

After taking up residency in the lawless Nueces strip, Fisher deserted the side of law and order and joined forces with the rustlers to become engaged in disposing of cattle and horses stolen in Mexico. This criminal activity led to considerable violence. Fisher was arrested several times by Texas Rangers and is reported to have been charged with eleven murders but never convicted.

Having a "clean" record, Fisher was appointed deputy sheriff of Uvalde County in 1883. It is written that in Fisher's territory he was respected and feared. A certain road branch bore the sign "This is King Fisher's road. Take the other!" It is said the advice seldom went unheeded. The gaudily dressed gunslinger was assassinated in a San Antonio vaudeville theater March 11, 1884.

Part III

Texas Family Secrets

*W*hen a family has a member or an incident it is not very proud of and that generally is not talked about in public conversation, it is often referred to as "one of the skeletons in our family closet." Not very pretty to look at and personally not very appetizing to talk about, we keep the skeletons shut away in the darkest closets we can create in our minds. Texas, as grand as it is and as perfect as we offer it up when we exercise our bragging rights, has the distinct if faint sounds of rattling bones in the dark recesses of her closets. This section of trivia is devoted to introducing a few of these less than brag-worthy incidences that have reared their ugly heads in our glorious growing up!

Vigilantism in 1910 Dallas

I was a deputy sheriff for Dallas County in the 1950s when I first heard vague stories about a black man being hanged from a second-story window of Dallas' "old red" courthouse across the street from the Sheriff's Office. It was not until forty years later that I heard the full story of this un-Dallas-like family secret. The full story is the exact reason we keep our family secrets hidden like skeletons in a closet—They are ugly!

It is to be remembered that at this time Dallas was home to Ku Klux Klan Chapter 66, largest in the country. Among its members were "pillars of the community" such as lawyers, judges, policemen, and other prominent citizens. The Klan's strength is underscored by the fact that in 1922 a prominent Dallas dentist was elected Grand Wizard of the Klan.

The 1910 mob lynching I was told about involved a sixty-eight-year-old black man, Allen Brooks, who was accused of raping a three-year-old white girl. It was alleged that Brooks was found in a barn with the girl, who was reported as missing. Brooks was to have been tried for the alleged offense, when a lynch-mob mentality took over. According to reports, the vigilantes knew they could find Brooks at his trial in the Dallas County courthouse on Main and Houston Streets.

Although a phalanx of officers were stationed at the courthouse, the mob overwhelmed them and made their way to the second-floor courtroom of Judge Robert Sealy, where the prisoner was easily overpowered and one end of a rope was slipped around his neck. The other end was thrown through an open window to the mob waiting two floors below. The victim was pushed and pulled through the open window. Although some said he was killed in the fall, contemporary reports say that Brook's body was dragged by the angry crowd to the corner of Elm and Akard Streets where he was hanged on a telephone pole—all this to the jeers and cheers of hundreds of Dallasites who watched the action. Although hundreds witnessed the entire event, as was often the case in vigilante actions, no one could be found who could or would identify the perpetrators. One thing is for sure. Despite doubts as to his guilt of the alleged crime, Brooks never got his day in court!

Some Cowardly Secrets Hid Behind Masks

A blight on society, including early Texas, were the secret terrorist-like organizations that sprang up in the South, Texas included, during the Reconstruction days following the Civil War, and which spilled over into the early decades of the twentieth century. The first such shameful organization one might think of is the highly publicized Ku Klux Klan. This secret organization, sometimes known as "the Invisible Empire," founded in 1865 in Pulaski, Tennessee, took its name from the Greek word "kuklos," meaning circle. It originally directed its attention toward the Republican Reconstruction government (both white and Negro), which they regarded as oppressive. They resented the rise of men who were former slaves to positions of equality. Attired in white robes or sheets and masks topped with pointed hoods, they terrorized officials to drive them out of office. Although centered in what was known as the "Deep South," the Klan had spread to Texas by 1868 and 1869.

Few Klan chapters existed in Texas after March of 1869, when the Grand Wizard of the order proclaimed the Klan disbanded. There were, however, reports of Klan activity in the Nacogdoches area in 1870. One newspaper reported that a Klan parade was held in McKinney in 1871.

The same paper reported that masked men had beaten a white teacher in a colored school in Bastrop County. The Congress passed the Ku Klux Klan Act of April 1871 and the Klan, in general, ceased to exist.

Perhaps the ugliest Klan-related secrets in Texas were generated by the Ku Klux Klan of the 1920s. This organization grew out of the unrest following World War I. The organization took the costume and name of the post Civil War organization. Its members paraded in Texas towns and cities, and crosses were burned in pastures as warnings to their targets for violence! The Klan, or Klan imposters, attempted to reform society with whips and other tools of violence, including tarring and feathering of people they wished to drive from their midst. Lynching and other forms of murder were used when warnings failed.

The Kleagles, or promoters, of the organization recruited Texans as members by the thousands. Although they did not always allow themselves to become involved in the acts of violence, many prominent citizens became members, hidden behind their robes and masks. One of the most blatant displays of this shameful organization in Texas was "Klan Day" at the State Fair of Texas in Dallas. At this 1923 convocation of the Klan, according to a history of the State Fair of Texas, the Klan initiated 5,631 new members before a crowd numbering 25,000. The secret organization, dressed in full Klan regalia, paraded before the mass under the watchful eye of former Dallas dentist Hiram W. Evans, who had been elected Grand Wizard of the Klan the previous year. According to the State Fair history, crosses burned as crusaders sang "Onward

Christian Soldiers." Festivities ended with a parade downtown. Although the Grand Wizard emphatically denied involvement in floggings, he used his State Fair forum to preach a message of hate, which emphasized that three groups were absolutely unblendable into the American way of life. They were the Negroes, Jews, and Catholics. By this time, their shameful conduct had resulted in numerous anti-Klan organizations springing up throughout the state.

The Ku Klux Klan started to decline in 1924 after its candidate for governor of Texas had been defeated. The Klan's demise was not solely due to their gubernatorial defeat at the polls. Many district attorneys were starting to prosecute Klansmen involved in violence.

Not so well known as the Ku Klux Klan was another secret order that enjoyed some success in Texas, the Knights of the White Camellia. Although they denied any connection with the organization, the highly secret group was confused as being part of the Ku Klux Klan. As their name graphically implies, this was an organization of white men pledged to support the supremacy of the white race and to oppose the mixing of the races. They resented the political encroachment of the carpetbaggers. It was their objective to restore white control of government. They did not employ such spectacular methods of violence as the Klan. As they met their objectives, the Knights were gradually disbanded.

Professional Revenge Reveals Family Secret

The recent death (10-2-98) of Orvon Grover Autry (better known as Gene Autry) reminded us of a bit of lore (considered as fact by locals) that reveals a penny-ante but classical example of a Texas family secret. Born September 27, 1907, in Tioga, Texas, located about an hour's drive north of Dallas, Autry in 1936 made an offer to spend the necessary funds to rejuvenate his ailing birthplace. His desire was that the town, which had been noted for its mineral springs, change its name to Autry Springs.

Tiogans shunned the singing cowboy's suggestion and his request to be immortalized on the Texas map. It is said that city fathers, at the urging of local physician E. Eugene Ledbetter, from whom, it is said, Autry got his first name, "Gene," rejected Autry's suggestion. It is reported the doctor was bitter because the sharecropper Autry family hadn't paid the doctor's fee for the delivery of the future film and recording star, said to have been the sum of $25. The singing cowboy had to settle for his memory being preserved by the Oklahoma town of Berwyn, where he grew up as a youth. The town, in 1941, voted to change its name to Gene Autry, Oklahoma.

His Tioga birthplace did honor him with a street bearing his name. Although only a $25 family secret, the Autry family's failure to pay the doctor's delivery fee cost the cowboy and the town of Tioga a more prominent place in the annals of Texas history.

Houston's Closely Guarded Secret

A secret that biographers of Sam Houston have failed to reveal, if they ever knew, has been nagging our collective curiosities since the Texas general became a public figure in Texas in 1835.

After being elected governor of Tennessee on January 1, 1829, Houston married Eliza H. Allen, the daughter of a prominent citizen of Gallatin, Tennessee. On April 16, when the marriage was only weeks old, the new Mrs. Houston returned to her parents, and Houston resigned as governor and left by steamer for Little Rock, Arkansas.

After several years of involvement with Indian affairs, he took an Indian wife, Tiana Rogers. In 1822 he joined with others in applying for a grant of land in Texas. He made his first trip to Texas in 1832 and returned to Texas to attend the convention of 1833.

If Sam Houston ever revealed the secret of what prompted his bride to return home to her parents, his secret remained held in the close confidence of those with whom he shared it. This family secret is one of the most closely guarded of any public figure in Texas history.

Texas' Unkindest Insult

What most Texans would consider "fightin' words" are attributed to Gen. Phillip H. Sheridan. The general, following the Civil War, was in 1867 made Military Governor of the Fifth Military District consisting of Louisiana and Texas. On July 30, 1867, after removing several Texas officials from office "because they were detriments to Reconstruction," Sheridan's harsh policies of Reconstruction met with the disapproval of President Andrew Johnson, who removed Sheridan from office as a tyrant. Perhaps influenced by his being stationed in Texas, Sheridan is attributed with making the statement, "If I owned Hell and Texas, I'd live in Hell and rent Texas out!"

"The Great Hanging"

The largest mass hanging by a "duly constituted court" involved the hanging of thirty-nine residents of the Confederate State of Texas in Gainesville in October 1862. The *Handbook of Texas* tells us the "great hanging" grew out of an alleged "Peace Party conspiracy," which prompted Confederate authorities to suppress it. The military authorities penetrated a secret organization said to number several hundred men.

On October 1, 1862, armed forces carried out raids in Cooke County and took sixty to seventy men into custody, bringing them to Gainesville and placing them under guard. On the same day, Col. William C. Young, commander of the Texas Cavalry, presided over a meeting. He created a "citizen's court" which was instructed to examine all crimes and offenses committed, determine the guilt or innocence of the accused, and pronounce appropriate punishment. The courts, in the succeeding weeks, found guilty thirty-nine of those charged and sentenced them to be hanged. The sentences were carried out in Gainesville.

Cannibals of Texas

Incredible as it sounds, the Lone Star State was once home to a cannibalistic tribe (at least cannibalistic in ceremonial setting). The Karankawa Indians, who occupied a strip of islands along the Texas coast and the mainland opposite from Galveston to Corpus Christi, were the most primitive of native cultures in Texas. They are alleged to have eaten dead or dying enemies in ceremonial fashion. Some historians have written that cannibalism might have been the way the Indians dealt with their prisoners of war.

The Karankawas fought with the men under pirate Jean Lafitte.

Jim Bowie's Tarnished Side

Hard as it might be for some of us to believe, our Alamo hero Jim Bowie had what one might easily call a tarnished side. Although it doesn't take away from the brilliant gleam of his heroics during our fight for independence, it was, nevertheless, a side of his character not considered an attribute by many. Bowie, along with his brother, Rezin Bowie, smuggled slaves into the United States after they were stolen from slave ships captured by freebooter Jean Lafitte (Lafitte never called himself a pirate).

Texans Lay Claim to Largest Train Heist

A family of latter-day owlhoots from Callahan County, Texas, who, in the 1920s, replaced galloping horses and bandannas with automobiles and nitroglycerine, were responsible for the largest train heist in U.S. history. The Newton Boys, who robbed scores of banks from Texas to Canada, seized three million dollars in 1924 from the C.M. & St. P. train near Chicago, before they dissolved and resorted to honest work.

In Texas Joe Newton was an excellent bronc rider and his brother Willis, the gang's mastermind, worked for a Uvalde banker and former governor, Dolph Briscoe. Briscoe once described Willis as "a gentleman." The Newton brothers lived to a ripe old age. Jess died in 1960, Doc died in 1974, Willis lived until 1979, and Joe died in 1989.

The Houstons' Separate Burials

When Texas hero General Sam Houston died at Huntsville in 1863, he was buried at his home there. Upon his death, his wife Margaret moved to Independence, Texas, to be near family. Upon her death in 1867 she was not buried next to her husband, but at Independence. This unusual arrangement came about due to a practice of that day. Mrs. Houston died of yellow fever, a scourge at the time. The disease was so feared that the deceased were put into the ground as soon as possible to prevent spread of the disease! This terrible disease resulted in the historical couple being separated in death.

Island Vice Post Office Street, Galveston's Notorious Vice District

Unflattering as it is, it is a fact of life that every major seaport around the world has its vice district. This is home to bars, brothels, burlesque houses, and the like. The Texas port of Galveston is no exception. In a city like Galveston there is always a certain amount of vice. It would be expected. But! in the boom recovery after the Civil War, with plenty of young soldiers in town, prostitution blossomed as never before. A vice district of saloons, bawdy houses, and variety shows formed around Post Office Street where, according to police Captain J.M. Riley, "Young men developed a taste for liquor and the nude adornments of the variety stage." This notorious vice district, probably the best known in Texas, remained a feature of the city for a hundred years.

These carvings found in the historic Waxahachie County courthouse are the handiwork of the Italian stonecutter whose amorous pursuit of Mable Frame, a local resident, was rejected. The spurned suitor had used Miss Frame as his model for the carvings. After being rejected, the Italian continued to use Mable's face, but made her more grotesque. (Photo by Marianne Cannon)

Hell Hath No Fury Like a Spurned Italian

Although it's not a family secret of the state of Texas, if you happened to be a member of the Frame family of Waxahachie at the turn of the nineteenth century, surely you would have felt some shame each time you passed the beautiful Ellis County courthouse in that city. For you would have known that the grotesque faces peering down from atop the columns of the facade of the seat of government were those of a family member.

Local history tells us that the Italian stone carver employed to sculpt the columns of the 1896 courthouse and who boarded with the Frame family in that city fell in love with the Frame's daughter, Mable. He used Mable Frame as a model for the faces he carved on the facade of the courthouse. When Mable spurned his affections, he continued carving her face but made them progressively uglier. So, today, the distorted face of Mable Frame peers down from its lofty perch atop the columns of one of the state's most beautiful courthouses.

Texas' Tarnished Badges Among Family Secrets

Few things are as reprehensible in the eyes of law-abiding Texans in the twentieth century as an officer of the law who turns his back on his sworn duty and finds himself on the opposite side of the law he swore to uphold! This, history reveals to us, was not necessarily the case in nineteenth-century Texas. Strange as it seems, coming on the heels of the prudish Victorian era, Texas produced or fell victim to some of the most loathsome maggots who ever tarnished the badge of the lawman. Chalk it up to weakness of character of the men or the toughness of the mentality of the times, that period of Texas history from the end of the Civil War until the dawning of the new century was soiled with lawmen who proved to be the dregs of humanity!

It didn't take much research to come up with enough examples to make a West Texas buzzard puke! These men and their ilk are truly fit to be called a Texas family secret! Appropriately, most of them, as though a part of God's plan of retribution, met their end in a violent and lethal manner!

One of the least publicized villains who had a stint hiding behind a badge was Ben Thompson. Born in 1843 in England, Thompson reflected a violent streak at an early age. His family moved to Austin, Texas, when he was a child. When Ben was a mere thirteen years old he deliberately shot and wounded a playmate. He was tried but not imprisoned. His violent side showed itself again in New Orleans when he killed a man in a knife duel. After escaping New Orleans he returned to Austin.

When the Civil War broke out, fighting for the Confederates gave rise to other crimes of personal violence. Thompson went to Mexico to fight for Maximilian. After returning to Austin, a murder there led to a prison term. Later in Austin, Thompson became city marshal. His skill with a gun made him effective in reducing the crime rate in that city.

In San Antonio Thompson got into an argument with the owner of a vaudeville theater and shot the man dead. He was once again tried and acquitted. But the case was far from being concluded! Two years later Thompson and another lawman of ill repute, J. "King" Fisher, returned to the theater where both men died in a fusillade of bullets fired by friends of the murdered theater owner. The assassins had effectively rid the state of two of its tarnished badges!

The second man filled with vengeful lead, Mr. John "King" Fisher, was another tarnished badge worth adding to our list of skeletons in our Texas closet. Details of his life are laid out in the chapter entitled "Minor Luminaries." We will note, however, that this renegade lawman worked just long enough as a gunman for a justice of the peace, helping to quell cattle rustling, to learn how profitable this criminal venture could be. He then started rustling stock for himself. During the 1870s he was the scourge of the Rio Grande border. Although accused and suspected in a dozen murders, he avoided conviction. With his "clean" record he was appointed deputy sheriff of Uvalde County. Like other "wolves-in-sheep's clothing," Fisher, as we have revealed, died with Ben Thompson at the hands of assassins in San Antonio.

Another product of the lawlessness of Texas at the close of the nineteenth century was Constable John Selman, ironically best remembered as the slayer of badman John Wesley Hardin. Selman began his violent career as a member of a vigilante group with the reputation of meting out "death-on-the-spot" sentences to rustlers who were unfortunate enough to fall into their hands. Selman himself didn't come to the necktie parties with totally clean hands. He, too, had engaged in his share of rustling cattle, which he butchered and sold. In 1876 Selman became deputy sheriff under Sheriff John Larn, where he helped the lawman break up a band of rustlers. After Sheriff Larn got a contract to sell beef to the army at Fort Griffin, there was a rumor that Larn and his deputy were butchering stolen cattle. Sheriff Larn was arrested and brought to Albany, Texas, where he was killed by vigilantes, but Selman escaped to West Texas. It is said that he was undaunted by his flirtation with the rope and continued his rustling enterprise.

Despite his several brushes with the law, in 1882 Selman turned up in El Paso serving as a peace officer once again. Selman's claim to historic fame was also his undoing! In 1895 Selman, hearing that the infamous gunslinger John Wesley Hardin had threatened him, walked into the Acme Saloon where Hardin was gambling. The constable with the tarnished badge placed two neat holes in the back of Hardin's evil head! Constable Selman, claiming that

Hardin had seen his reflection in the mirror behind the bar, had attempted to draw on him, and that he shot in self-defense. He was acquitted, but a year later he was killed by a deputy U.S. marshal.

Part IV

More "Truth is Stranger Than Fiction!"

As we said in our first Texas trivia offering, "When we hear a story that is too bizarre to believe yet we learn that it is indeed true, we are prone to say, 'Truth is stranger than fiction!'" Although our first book offered a cornucopia of such stories about the Lone Star State, there are still an abundance of incredible but true stories that deserve capturing in print. This section includes some of them.

Paris, Texas' Eiffel Tower became distinctively Texan recently with the addition of a gargantuan red cowboy hat. (Photo by Marianne Cannon)

Paris' Eiffel Tower Receives Traditional Texas Topping

We might not be bustin' new sod if we told you that the North Texas city of Paris had its own Eiffel Tower, second in size only to that of its European namesake. The 65-foot tower stands next to the Love Civic Center on the corner of Jefferson Rd. and S. Collegiate Dr. What is new and, we think noteworthy, is that in October of 1998 this Texas city's Eiffel Tower was topped by what is, no doubt, one of the state's largest cowboy hats. The red hat is so large that it took three gallons of "fire-engine" red paint and three hours to paint it. This unusual addition to the Paris skyline will surely be added to the Chamber of Commerce's already large list of scenic attractions. We think it is a must-see during one's evening in Paris. We are grateful to the *Paris News* for their permission to let us use excerpts from their coverage of this topping off of the tower.

The Texas Ghost that Lived in Opulence

Although Texas has about as many ghost stories as a prickly pear has spines, none of the ethereal visitors from the great beyond have lived in the opulence of the ghost in the story you are about to read. Although several historians have made reference to this wispy visitor to the world of the living who resided in Austin, his story has eluded most Texans.

We have given ample print to such beings as the ghost who haunts San Antonio's Circus Museum; Dallas' "Lady of the Lake," who surfaces periodically from White Rock Lake to make believers of the most circumspect of skeptics; the mischievous saints who keep employees of Waxahachie's Catfish Plantation on their toes; "the ghost of Bragg Road" in the Big Thicket; and the visitors from the spirit world who are said to be in residence at the Excelsior Hotel in Jefferson. But none of these can lay claim to living in such opulence as the ghost who is said to occupy the Governor's Mansion in our state capital.

We have to concede that these are pretty impressive digs for someone, or something, who may not exist at all! The story of this nebulous visitor to the state house residence of Texas governors begins during the Civil War administration of one of the state's little-known governors, Pendleton Murrah. Sources at the mansion tell us that the governor and his wife were visited at the mansion by a young nephew and niece. The legend of the ghost says that the man fell in love with the young lady (who was not his sibling). It is said that he proposed marriage and after she insultingly rejected his proposal, the young man shot himself to death rather than live without his newfound love. The household arose to find the lifeless body of the young man lying across the blood-soaked bed. One writer reported that from this time on, servants avoided this particular bedroom in the mansion after the young man's ghost appeared. The suicide of this young relative provides the basis for the ghost story of the official residence of Texas governors, the Governor's Mansion.

Administrators at the mansion told us that in the past years they know of no one who has seen manifestations of the ghost, nor do any staff members avoid the bedroom involved on that fateful day, although the room still exists. An inquiry to Governor George Bush as to whether his family had witnessed any evidence of the mansion's being haunted produced a reply, a part of which is as follows: "The room was eventually converted into a closet and two baths, and it remains so today. Fortunately, we have neither seen nor heard from Murrah's nephew since we have lived in the house. The only creatures which tiptoe through the house late at night—besides our daughters, who sometimes forget their curfew—are the family cats."

Baseball Star's Haunted Home

The *Dallas Morning News* edition of December 6, 1987, has a story relating how Waxahachie-born major-league baseball player Paul Richards, who was the former manager of the Baltimore Orioles and the Chicago White Sox, made Ripley's "Believe-It-Or-Not" column by pitching a shutout left-handed to lead his Waxahachie High School team in the state semifinals, only to pitch right-handed the next day to win the state championship.

This Victorian home in Waxahachie, Texas, was the birthplace of baseball great Paul Richards. It is now the popular restaurant Catfish Plantation, which is billed as a "haunted restaurant." (Photo by Marianne Cannon)

The baseball player's home is now a popular Waxahachie restaurant that has gained notoriety as a "haunted house." This is based on unexplained and unnatural happenings at the former home of the baseball star. The ghosts seem to be quite active if you are to believe reports given us recently by our waitress, Rhema Zufelt, a three-year employee of the restaurant. Rhema spoke quite openly about her "encounters," as she put it, with the spirit world, while working at the popular establishment. "On one occasion another employee and I drove past the restaurant when it was closed. We saw lights flashing inside, so we stopped and got out to watch. We both exclaimed excitedly when, through the window, we saw a man walk from one dining room to another dining room."

We asked Rhema if the man looked three-dimensional. She paused for a moment then said, reflectively, "Sort of, but somewhat hazy." Rhema told us that on another occasion she was looking out the window toward the parking lot when she saw a young woman in her late teens or early twenties, looking back at her through the window. She said she believed the woman to be Caroline, one of the three ghosts said to haunt the restaurant. Rhema said she had also witnessed some ghostly activities such as the vacuum cleaner coming on, although unplugged. She said she also witnessed a teacup fly off a shelf and hit a wall across the room. "One day," Rhema continued, "we all came to work after the restaurant had been closed and were surprised to find some freshly baked cobblers waiting for us in the kitchen." These manifestations qualify the Catfish Plantation as the most active of all the Texas ghosts we have investigated.

Seguin's "Whipping Oaks" Economical Measure or Part of Justice System?

As emphasized in John Gesick Jr.'s history of Seguin, *Under the Live Oak Tree*, "The oak tree is a cultural part of Seguin's history." In his artistically written history of the county seat of Guadalupe County, Mr. Gesick makes reference to several oak trees that are noteworthy in the city. While all have contributed in one measure or another to the city's history, the ones that piqued my interest because of their uniqueness were the city's "Whipping Oaks."

In collecting unusual facts about Texas, we have never ferreted out any tree used for meting out legal punishment save the numerous "hanging trees" (both legal and those of the "necktie party" variety), scattered around the state. Then, like many unusual facts, we discovered Seguin's "Whipping Oaks" tucked in a corner of a reference book. Author Gesick and the Seguin Public Library generously helped us fill in the blanks.

The "Whipping Oaks" are found on the north side of the fountain in Central Park. There is an iron ring embedded in one of the trees. This ring was supposedly used to tie persons who had been found guilty of a crime that was punishable by lashes to be dealt out by the court. A city fact sheet says that it probably had more publicity than actual use. Perhaps its presence and publicity was as much a deterrent to criminal acts as the public floggings. A similar ring is located in a tree on the west side of the square.

The city that was once called Walnut Springs apparently meant to give the oaks ample exposure to the results that could be expected if one ran afoul of the law. One historian infers that the Whipping Oaks were instituted as an economical measure: "Since jails were expensive commodities, Seguin had its 'Whipping Oaks'." The truth, however strange, is that at one time Texas turned to corporal punishment in a public setting, both as a punishment and as a lesson to young and old!

Frank James, Brother to Infamous Outlaw, Worked at Dallas' Sanger Brothers as Salesman

Alexander Franklin James, brother to Jesse James and part of the bank robbing, murdering James gang, strange as it seems, worked innocuously on the sales staff at Dallas' Sanger Brothers Department store.

In his book *Blood-Letters and Badmen*, Jay Robert Nash, in giving the history of the infamous James gang, informs us that Alexander Franklin James surrendered to Governor Crittenden on October 5, 1882. At age thirty-nine, Frank James was the last of the Jesse James gang. The Missouri governor, after promising James protection, had the outlaw jailed to await trial on several robbery and murder charges. After his acquittal, Frank James was freed and returned to his farm. He lived there until he died February 18, 1915.

Sometime during the 1880s Frank James made his way to Dallas. A manuscript written by a fellow worker indicates that Frank James, whom he described as "friendly and generous," was working in the Dallas store in the latter 1880s.

Two-Bits, Four-Bits, Six-Bits—it All Began in Texas

Although most of us are familiar with these expressions, few are aware that they originated right here in Texas. And even fewer know what one bit is. But, early Texans had to know, as the posted rate at ferries sometimes listed the rate for transporting a small animal, such as a pig, was "one bit." As coins were rare in early Texas, colonists used the Spanish silver dollar, known variously as "pieces of eight" and "Spanish-milled dollar." These coins could be cut into eight pie-shaped pieces known as "bits." Each piece was worth twelve and one-half cents in U.S. currency. When the United States coined the quarter it was worth twenty-five cents or "two bits." The half-dollar was worth four bits, etc.

The "pieces of eight" of Texas history was the first coin used by Texas colonists. Also known as the Spanish milled dollar or pillar dollar, it was the forerunner of our own silver dollar. The coin could be cut into eight pieces called bits. Each bit was worth twelve and one-half cents American.

Llano Estacado in Fact and Fiction

Llano Estacado is described in the Texas State Historical Association's *Handbook of Texas* as "one of the most perfect plains regions in the world. It is a high plateau which extends from the central western parts of Texas northward over most of the Panhandle of Texas and westward into eastern New Mexico." Although this description is vague, it provides the average Texan with a reasonable overview of the area under consideration. The *Handbook* also informs us that the name is translated into English as "Staked Plain." The Spanish word *llano* (pronounced yano) means plain.

Although there are several explanations as to why the Spanish explorers gave the plains this name, one that is widely accepted has to do with the land's topography. Four hundred years ago when explorers traversed the plains, that region was a treeless sea of waving grass that was belly high on their mounts. As there were no landmarks by which they could navigate, it is said that lance-like wooden stakes were brought to be driven into the ground to be used as trail markers.

Because of the scarcity of surface water, the land was shunned by both buffalo and Indians until encroaching settlers in the lower areas forced them on to it. The arrival of the vast herds of buffalo brought new inhabitants on the llano. Buffalo hunters came to pursue the animals for their valuable hides. The lush grasslands became tempting to ranchers, who visualized their herds grazing on what seemingly was interminable pastureland. In the late nineteenth century few Texans south of the "High Plains," as we called it, knew much about what was one of the state's largest pieces of real estate, especially its topography and its people.

Across the Atlantic millions of German boys in the 1880s and 1890s were eagerly gorging their minds and hearts with detailed (albeit fictional) introductions to the Texas High Plains, including its people and their culture. They waited breathlessly for the next episode in the lives of the German frontiersman "Old Shatterhand" and his faithful and trusted friend "Winnetou," a young, elegant, intelligent Mescalero Apache with whom he had bonded.

Meredith McClain Ph.D. writing in the *Lubbock Magazine* tells us that both of these characters were conceived in the fertile imagination of German author Karl May, the most successful German writer in terms of lasting popularity and profit.

May was born in the German state of Saxony in 1842. Texas was still a frontier republic at that time. McClain points out that the setting of Mays books about the American West, which made the author a millionaire, was on the Llano Estacado. Dr. McClain writes: "Standing (or riding) tall beside 'Old Shatterhand' it is Winnetou who, representing the most noble attributes of the Native American, completely wins the hearts and the imaginations of his German readers."

His mention of "a forest of cactus" betrays to us today the fact that the German writer—capturing his German readers' hearts with his first-person narrative, sprinkled generously with imagined exotic descriptions of a landscape and a people he had never seen—never set foot on the Llano Estacado. One must remember that Texas was, at the time of May's writing, an exciting new frontier. Foreign hearts, especially those beating in the young, impressionable boys who represented most of Karl May's readership, were ripe for being exposed to cowboy and Indian stories on distant shores.

We are grateful to Meredith McClain for letting us share her overview of her beloved Llano Estacado, both the fact and the fiction.

Move Over Chicago—Make Room for Texas Wind

The *1998-1999 Texas Almanac*, published by the *Dallas Morning News*, informs us that "Texas is the tornado capital with an average of 126 tornadoes touching down in Texas each year." Naturally, as is the case with many records, the state's vast size is a factor. The book, on which we rely for many facts, goes on to astound us with one particular "big wind" fact. "The greatest outbreak of tornadoes on record in Texas is associated with Hurricane Beulah in September 1967. Within a five-day period, September 19-23, 115 known tornadoes, all in Texas, were spawned by this great hurricane. Sixty-seven occurred on September 20, a Texas record for a single day."

The Great White Comfort: The Monument for Child's Play That Became a Memorial to the Wife of its Originator

We went to the historic Evergreen Cemetery in Paris, Texas, to gather information on some of the cemetery's best-known grave markers. This old cemetery, which has a population of 40,000 in a city of a population of 26,000, is well known for its elaborate grave markers. Jim Blassingame directed us to the markers about which we had inquired. He then told us of the cemetery's newest addition to its more elaborate grave markers, a "huge white buffalo, big as your car," Jim said.

We easily found the big white buffalo, sculpted by Harold Clayton from a seven-ton block of West Texas white limestone, on a small hill near the cemetery's southeast corner. An article in the *Paris News* reported that carving the buffalo took 400 hours. Hamp Hodges along with his wife Elizabeth "Buffy" designed the monument for kids to

The bright afternoon sun illuminates the features of the huge Texas lime-stone buffalo that is now a memorial to "Buffy" Hodges, who is buried a few feet away. The monument, which she helped design, was designed for children to play on. (Photo by Marianne Cannon)

play on. In Hodges' words, "I wanted kids to understand that death does not have to be a bad thing." Hodges commissioned the work adding, "As a child I used to come to this cemetery to visit the graves of my grandparents. I remember it as an open place to play." Why a buffalo? "We raise buffalo and my wife's nickname is 'Buffy' and my corporate logo is a buffalo."

Here the story takes on an air of poignancy. Although Hodges' wife Buffy helped design the monument and saw it during its creation, she never saw it installed. Buffy died of cancer on February 13, 1999, six days after the buffalo was installed, and is buried a few feet from the enormous white buffalo she helped design. Hamp Hodges told us the monument that was designed for kids to play on is now "a memorial to Buffy and the marker for the Hodges family burial plot."

We are grateful to the *Paris News* for permitting us to use excerpts from their article about the white buffalo monument.

Texas Forest of Dwarfs

Standing in a state whose very name infers bigness is an incongruous phenomenon. In a state which boasts over 200 trees on the Texas Forest Service's "Big Tree" list of state and national champion trees, judged largely on size, is a forest of oak trees that seldom reach more than three feet in height. These dwarf oaks, overshadowed by their big

brothers on the "Big Tree" list, are Havard Oaks, which put down roots ninety feet into the Texas soil, prompting some to theorize that the oaks are "growing in the wrong direction." These strange but true oaks may be seen in the Monahans Sandhills State Park off Interstate 20 west of Odessa, Texas.

Initials Can be Confounding Without History Lesson

Visitors who drive in Houston or newly arrived residents may well be confused by the name of one of the city's busiest streets. The street bears only the initials O.S.T. Why, one might ask himself, would a city name a street only with initials? A few well-meaning locals might give you an answer that is only partially correct. "The street is named for the Old Spanish Trail" also known as "Camino Real" or "King's Highway." This is true, the street draws attention to an important part of our Texas history. The Camino Real was blazed in 1691 by the provincial governor of Texas, as a direct route from Monclova, then capital of the province, to the Spanish missions that had been established among the Indians of East Texas. Moses Austin traversed the trail en route to San Antonio to request an impresario grant from the Spanish government in 1820. Many Anglo-American colonists traveled this road to the interior of Texas.

In 1929 the Texas Legislature passed an act establishing a state highway designated to preserve and maintain the route of the Old Spanish Trail. But don't feel that by driving on Houston's O.S.T. you are traveling the same route of your earlier Texas forefathers. The Houston Public Library tells us that the street was only named for this historical transportation route and does not follow the course of the Camino Real or the state highway of the 1920s.

German Ingenuity

The Kendall County town of Comfort is the setting of an unusual event that occurred about two years after its founding. The town was founded by German settlers from New Braunfels in 1854. The town was in possession of a cannon, which was to be fired in the event of an emergency to which the town should be alerted. Intended to alert citizens to Indian attack, fire, or other emergency, the cannon became useful in solving another serious if somewhat unorthodox emergency, according to local historian, Greg Krauter.

Mr. Krauter told us that in preparation for Comfort's celebration of the Fourth of July a wagonload of beer had been ordered from the Menger Brewery in San Antonio. The wagon, however, arrived two days early, and not being pasteurized and there being no cold storage in those days, the cannon was fired to draw the citizens into town and alert them to what for Germans would be a catastrophe, the loss of a wagon of beer!

Mr. Krauter said there was a minor uprising of the citizens because by definition, the cannon shot was a false alarm. When faced with the situation, the Germans rose to the occasion and solved the problem in a most logical way. They celebrated Fourth of July on the second of July and drank the beer before it could spoil!

Keene, Texas, Better Do Your Shopping on Sunday

Just south of Dallas is the Johnson County town of Keene. This is a town with business habits unique in Texas. Founded in 1893 by Seventh Day Adventists wishing to establish a school in a rural setting, the town of Keene grew up around the campus of Keene Industrial Academy. Due to their religious beliefs, says local historian Mary Ann Hadley, "as a general rule, business in Keene is conducted on Sunday, as its businesses are closed from sundown on Friday until Sunday morning. Shopping is done on Sunday." The Keene post office is closed both Saturday and Sunday. This arrangement fits snugly into the plans of Adventists, who make up a majority of the town's residents. The town, it is believed, was named for a friend of an early postmaster.

Ransom Canyon or (Canon de la Rescate)

Southeast of the city of Lubbock, Texas, on the Brazos River in the vicinity of Yellow House Canyon, one can find one of the most unique links to the Native Americans in Texas—Ransom Canyon. This canyon on the Texas South Plains came by its name quite honestly. According to the book *El Llano Estacado*, the canyon was known by the 1820s as a place where the Indians and New Mexicans met to barter for cattle and horses and trade for any captives. Captives were literally ransomed. These meetings took place from July to September each year, and the practice continued into the 1840s.

Corpus Christi's Ocean-Going Ghost

Basking in the Gulf Coast surf and enjoying a well-earned rest, after serving for thirty-nine years as a maritime war machine, is one of Corpus Christi's most visited tourist attractions, the U.S.S. *Lexington*, or "Lady Lex" as she is fondly known. This nemesis of the Japanese fleet and air forces during WW II is located on Corpus Christi beach next to the Texas State Aquarium. Dubbed the "Blue Ghost" by Tokyo Rose in a broadcast, because the enemy reported her sunk at least twice, the giant aircraft carrier, while certainly no ghost, is reportedly haunted!

During our visit we found the floating city's "battleship gray" hulk anything but an apparition. But then we did not permit ourselves to wander below decks to the innermost bowels of the historic warship, where strange goings-on have been reported. People touring the decks below have asked about the sailor they encountered lurking in the shadows of the passageways. Those folks sighting the sailor reported that he didn't speak, and he was there one second and gone the next. Was he the spirit of an unrecovered sailor who was a victim of the carrier's torpedo hit or the kamikaze strike?

Inquires about the ethereal crewmember were not limited to one somewhat spooky tourist. On more than one occasion the sightings were questioned. But the sightings of the lone sailor have not been the "haunted" ship's only manifestation of Lady Lex's ghost. Strange things like heavy steel doors, or hatches, as we ex-sailors say, closing on their own lend an added air of apprehension in the minds of some of the ship's present staff, none of whom have seen the lone sailor.

Haunted or not, this magnificent defender of America's freedom warrants a visit!

Hico's Brushy Bill Roberts Alias Billy the Kid

A marker can be found in the Hamilton County town of Hico that recalls one of the town's residents who claimed to be Billy the Kid. Mr. Bob Hefner, a local historian, has spent a number of years studying the claim and touting its

The city of Hico remembers "Brushy Bill" Roberts with this downtown marker. The text reads "Ollie L. 'Brushy Bill' Roberts, alias Billy the Kid died in Hico, Texas December 27, 1950. He spent the last days of his life trying to prove to the world his true identity and obtain the pardon promised him by the governor of the state of New Mexico. We believe his story and pray to God for the forgiveness he solemnly asked for."

validity. He told us that the Hamilton County resident was born William Henry Roberts in Cranfills Gap, Texas. According to Robert's claim, when his mother died he went to live with his Aunt Kathrine Bonney. While living with her he took to using the name Bill Bonney, which, it is said, was the Kid's real name. He said later he was known as "Billy the Kid."

When we asked Mr. Hefner about Bonney coming from the streets of New York, he said, "That was a story created by a writer to give some romanticism to the Billy the Kid story." Hefner said he never met Brushy Bill but knew his story well. Roberts claimed that when his father went into the Civil War he drifted into New Mexico, arriving just in time for the famed Lincoln County wars. He later returned to Texas to live with his father.

Mr. Hefner said Robert's past as Billy the Kid was not known to the folks of Hico until it was reported on the wire services when he asked the governor of New Mexico for a pardon. Brushy Bill's death at age ninety-one in Hico in 1950 put an end to his claim to Old West notoriety! There are folks in Hico today who believe Bill's story.

Vanity Trips Up "Wild Bunch"

While being pursued by law posses as well as being dogged by the Pinkerton Detectives, wild west outlaws Butch Cassidy and Harry Longabaugh, known as "The Sundance Kid," along with others who made up the bank and train robbing gang known variously as "The Hole-in-the-Wall Gang" and the "Wild Bunch," headed for Fort Worth, Texas, where they holed up at Fannie Porter's brothel.

While laying low in the bustling cow town, patronizing such places as the White Elephant Saloon, they strolled the

This dapper group of notorious outlaws are Butch Cassidy (far right) and the Sundance Kid (far left) and the "Hole-in-the-Wall Gang." This photo almost got them arrested in Fort Worth.

town's street and took in its pleasures. One day they passed a photographer's studio, and feeling pretty cocky, no doubt, they had a group portrait made. The photographer was so proud of his handiwork that he posted a copy of the photo in his window as an example of his fine work. This led to the undoing of the notorious gang. A Pinkerton detective strolling the streets of Fort Worth noticed the photo of his quest, and after learning more about its time frame, alerted local lawmen to the presence of the "Wild Bunch" in their fair city.

The subsequent flurry of excitement resulted in the much-sought-after gang's flight into a questionable future! While some hold that the gang fled to South America where they were killed by local police, others claim that Cassidy, at least, returned to his place of birth in the western United States, where he lived out the remainder of his life!

A reminder of the presence of this infamous gang of outlaws, including their sitting for the photo that drove them deeper into the pages of the history books, is today's very modern business development in downtown Fort Worth, "Sundance Square." Ed Bass, its developer, had these historic exploits in mind when he named the new development.

Texas Immigrant and Ringling Bros. Circus Team Up to Make Fruitcake Popular

For over 100 years the Christmas holidays have been made tastier for uncountable families around the world by a delicacy of Texas origin. Most Texans are familiar with Deluxe fruitcake from Corsicana's Collins Street Bakery. Most will be surprised to know that the success of this popular holiday cake can be contributed to the Ringling Brothers Circus!

The year 1896 was a decidedly special year for fruitcake connoisseurs. It was in that year that Texas immigrant Gus Weidmann, a master baker from Wiesbaden, Germany, teamed up with Tom McElwee in Corsicana, Texas, to establish the Collins Street Bakery and create the Deluxe fruitcake now distributed worldwide. A company history reveals that while Gus worked his magic in the kitchen,

Tom excelled at his forté, promoting the eye-appealing as well as palate-pleasing fruitcake.

By 1906 the demand of the bakery's clientele resulted in the bakery closing its original plant and opening a larger, more efficient facility. The new facility was of such an ambitious size that it allowed the partners to make the entire second floor into a hotel. Among those hosted by the bakery, to name but a few, were Will Rogers, Enrico Caruso, "Gentleman Jim" Corbett, and a guest who turned out to be one of the bakery's major benefactors, a man whose name is synonymous with circus, John Ringling of Ringling Brothers Circus. It was this man's hotel visit that put Collins Street Bakery in the mail order business, which is, next to its quality product, its real claim to fame. Old timers at the bakery remember when Ringling's entire circus traipsed over to the bakery and ordered cakes for families and friends all over the world. This single event began an international Christmas event that continues today!

The bakery, we were told, has a permanent staff of 60 which swells to 760 the first of October each year to bake and ship the four million pounds of fruitcake to the 198 foreign lands, as well as the multitude of cities across the United States.

The Texas Jail That Billy the Kid Broke Into

Although there are, for obvious reasons, precious few remaining newspaper accounts and no eyewitnesses to interview about the many exploits of the young man known to us today as Billy the Kid, volumes have been written based upon the legends left behind by his contemporaries. One of his chroniclers was his nemesis, Sheriff Pat Garrett. Many of these legends are based upon facts as remembered by those who lived in those headline-making days of the desperado who, it is said, killed twenty-one men before he was twenty-one years of age. Aficionados of Wild West outlaws remember his bloody escape from the Lincoln County, New Mexico jail, early in the afternoon of April 28, 1881, when he shot and killed two of Pat Garret's best guns, J.W. Bell and Bob Oilinger, after being shackled hand and foot and placed in a second-floor cell. But little has been written about the Kid's only recorded incident where he broke into jail, which just happened to be in Texas. The incident is recorded in Pat Garret's *Authentic Life of Billy the Kid* published in 1927.

The story of Billy the Kid's break-in of the El Paso County jail is truly a piece of Texas lore that is backed up by the Texas State Historical Association. To set the scene we must remind you that the small Mexican pueblo of San Elizario was El Paso's county seat from the time the county was established in 1850 until 1876. Around 1850 El Paso's first county jail was built. After "the Kid" had killed his second man he became a fugitive in Old Mexico.

While there he formed an alliance with Melguides Segura and Jesse Evans. After returning to New Mexico, Billy the Kid learned that his friend and partner in crime Segura had run afoul of the law and had been arrested in San Elizario and placed in jail there. The Kid learned that Segura might be in danger in that town. He decided to go to San Elizario and free Segura from custody.

According to Garret's story, it was the fall of 1876 that the Kid made the eighty-one-mile ride to the Rio Grande town. Traveling along the Rio Grande, he stopped briefly in El Paso, known then as Franklin, Texas. Upon arrival at the little San Elizario jail, he aroused the Mexican who was standing guard at the lock-up. He tricked the guard into opening the door "for some additional prisoners." He then grabbed the jailer's arm, and with the barrel of his revolver acting as a persuader, he convinced the guard to surrender his handgun and the keys to the jail. He and Segura shackled the two guards on duty to a post outside. They then locked the jail with its new prisoners and rode into the night!

More recent newspaper publicity about the jail would indicate it's being recognized as an important piece of Texas heritage. An article in the *El Paso Times* dated May 15, 1987, says that the city's historic Mission Trails Committee is dedicated to preserving the site as the only jail Billy the Kid broke *into.* This site is to be a tourist attraction, although 121 years have passed since William Bonney, alias Billy the Kid, broke into the Texas jail.

Legend of the White Buffalo

Of all the Texas legends that have been passed on from one generation to another, one of the most intriguing has almost been lost. It is the legend of the white buffalo. This legend comes from about as far north in Texas as is possible, Ochiltree County, in the Texas Panhandle. Legend has it that south of Perryton, the most northern of Texas' county seats, being only eight miles from the Oklahoma line, across Wolf Creek there existed a white bull buffalo that once roamed the country. Hunters, it is said, couldn't kill it and Indians couldn't touch it. The story goes that "as the buffalo herds thinned out, the white buffalo led one last stampede into a norther and was never seen again."

"Potterize" an Ominous Term with Ties to the Texas Navy

A term considered a household word on the frontier was "Potterize." This word was synonymous with emasculating a man. It had its origin with a former secretary of the Texas navy, Robert Potter. The term was coined when Potter, then a U.S. Congressman from North Carolina, took revenge on two of his wife's cousins, whom he suspected of having adulterous affairs with his wife. According to a biography of Robert Potter, the two cousins had a habit of visiting Potter's home on Sundays. One man was the Rev. Louis Taylor, minister of the Methodist church. The second cousin who fell victim to Potter's jealousy was seventeen-year-old Louis Wiley. On Sunday, Aug. 28, 1831, Potter attacked both men and, using his pocketknife, castrated both men or, as the biographer put it, "Potterized" them.

Marble Falls "The Blind Man's Town"

The Hill Country town of Marble Falls was founded in 1887 by Adam Rankin Johnson. Johnson had surveyed land in the area for the state in 1854. Johnson, who had attained the rank of general in the Civil War, was blinded in both eyes when shot in the face. When he returned to Texas after the war, he remembered the countryside around the falls on the Colorado River so vividly that he laid out the town site from memory with the help of his son, Robert. For years the town was known as "The blind man's town."

Texans Invent Rodeo

Although the scenario may be fictitious, the details and the results are as real as any other fact about the Lone Star

State. Few of the developing settlements of West Texas seemed to match the raw enthusiasm shown by the fast growing town of Pecos. This town was located so close to the river that was its namesake, that all a resident had to do was walk out his back door and river water would fill his boots.

While its nearness to the river may be exaggerated, its passion for cow country was not. Neither was its town folks' love for the July Fourth holiday! This was one day of the year when the dusty cow town could get all gussied up in seldom seen brightness. Every building took deep pride in draping the national colors over every available sign and post. The Fourth of July of 1883 proved to be a historical one, not only for the good folks of Pecos, but for those of us who love the pomp and excitement of the rodeo today.

As the town was preparing for the holiday celebration, the foreman of one of the county's largest spreads engaged in a heated debate as to which one of the men could rope and brand a yearling in the fastest time. The debate soon escalated into a full-blown argument with a bet of a ten-dollar gold piece riding on the result. The two, encouraged by bystanders, agreed to meet in the wagon yard behind the livery stable after the Fourth of July parade, where the bet would be decided with a real victim donated by the owner of the ranch where the first foreman worked. Several foremen of neighboring ranches, upon hearing of the test of cowboy skill, agreed to show up and judge the contest. Some of the working cowboys, having never heard of laying a half month's wages on one's working skill, began to fling challenges among themselves, like so much idle bragging. But idle they were not!

Each was accompanied by a wager ranging from $2 to a new Stetson. If the wagers were taken up, the wagon yard was going to be mighty full come Fourth of July. It was decided that all of the contests would be limited to the skills used in the ranch's annual roundup, or, as the Mexicans called it, *rodear*, the Spanish word for surround. By the time the cowpokes decided what skills they wanted to compete in, the entire gamut was represented. Those who fell short could already be heard taunting, "Just wait 'til next year!" This event in Pecos, Texas, in 1883 became known as the first rodeo, as it was called by the gringos, whose Spanish was less than perfect! The rodeo was to become an annual Fourth of July event. Not only in Pecos, but also in any town where the spirit of the West ran high.

Hidden Secrets of the "Ugly Old Goddess" of Austin

Hoisted to the top of the Texas capitol dome in February 1888, the monumental zinc statue known as "the goddess of liberty" remained on the state's symbol of government nearly ninety-eight years. The statue, which was painted white and which held aloft a gilded lone star, intrigued millions of visitors to the state capitol. The goddess stands nearly sixteen feet tall and weighs about one ton. The reason the statue, which to many was nameless, was so intriguing, according to a fact sheet provided by the Texas Memorial Museum in Austin, was because so little was known about its origin. Recent investigations have helped enlighten us as to the statue's history.

The goddess was, in all likelihood, inspired by the statue of freedom placed on the dome of the national capitol in 1863, and by the publicity about the Statue of Liberty under construction in New York in the 1870s. The statue was designed by capitol architect Elijah Myers of Detroit. The statue, because of its harsh countenance, inspired criticism at first. Because of her facial features, one local newspaper called her "Old Lady Goddess" saying that her face "resembles an old woman of eighty."

During restoration of the original statue, a decaying time capsule was discovered inside the five-pointed star originally held by the goddess. In addition to the remains of spiders, roaches, and winged insects was found a copy of *Texas Vorwaerts* (Texas Forward), a German-language newspaper printed in Austin, and two Wisconsin newspapers; as well as several business cards and a "broadside" (advertisement). The finding of the German-language newspaper confirmed a report made in 1946 by the late Edward Schultze of Austin, that in 1888 he and his future wife, Emma Wolfe, placed in the star a calling card and a copy of *Texas Vorwaerts*, the prominent German-language newspaper established by Schultze's father in 1883. These long hidden secrets of the goddess have been preserved for exhibition.

Phobia in the Plains

Although the dictionary defines "phobia" as a fear that is irrational, the folks in the South Plains city of Lubbock might cite you many concrete—and steel—reasons why their fear of renting an office in that city's Great Plains Life Building (now the Metro Towers) was anything but irrational! Lubbock took great pride in this twenty-story office building, rising like a steel and glass monolith out of the Texas Plains. Built between 1953 and 1955, the building was billed by local financiers as "The tallest structure between Fort Worth and Denver."

That was all before the fateful day of May 11, 1970, when a one-and-a-half-mile-wide killer tornado slammed through the heart of Lubbock, leaving twenty-six dead and conservatively two thousand injured, as well as damage to homes and businesses totaling $200 million. But, as if these statistics weren't enough to satisfy the appetite of this atmospheric beast, just as wall clocks froze at 9:46 P.M., giving mute testimony to the time of the ravaging storm, all interest in occupying the Great Plains Life Building also froze!

According to late workers in the structure, "The building swayed and twisted during the tornadic winds." Later, reports put the winds at 200 MPH. The horror stories recounted by those working in the building that fateful night read like a critic's review of one of today's computer enhanced disaster movies. "Everyone had to avoid the elevators, the lights were off. Everyone had to escape the building by walking down twenty flights of stairs through dust and falling plaster." One group that fled the structure said, in referring to the office building, "We couldn't imagine how long it would last!"

Walls were cracked by diagonal tension. Researchers reported that the building's steel frame suffered a twelve-inch permanent deformation. For days radio and television stations predicted the building would collapse. The physical damage to the pride of the Plains was not all that required repairing. Based upon all visible and reported evidence, local Lubbock businessmen's associations appealed to the city council to declare the building a nuisance and force the owners to repair or demolish it. One day before the structure was to go on the block in a sheriff's sale in 1974, Amarillo investors bought it.

After making repairs recommended by a Texas Tech study, the investors held a ribbon-cutting ceremony on Oct. 15, 1975. For five years the people of Lubbock were afraid to occupy the building for fear it might collapse. A 1990 local newspaper article indicated that 70 percent of the building's available space was occupied. Phobias with a concrete basis are slow to heal.

St. Elmo's Fire in Texas

Early Texas trail drivers, while herding the massive herds of Texas cattle over the historic trails of Texas, were sometimes treated, especially during storms, to a bizarre phenomenon in which eerie luminous flashes of yellow-green tongues of lightening-like fire arced from the horns of one steer to the horns of a nearby steer. Often this early day "laser show" continued until the entire herd was bathed in an incandescent glow. This phenomenon, although a mystery to the cowpokes of old, is today associated with ships' masts and aircraft. It is technically known as St. Elmo's Fire.

The World's Richest Acre

The city of Kilgore is located 120 miles east of Dallas on Interstate 20. Founded in 1871, it was a quiet agricultural center specializing in cotton and timber. It remained a quiet hub of agriculture until the discovery of the vast East Texas oil field in 1930. This discovery changed the history of the world and of Kilgore forever!

In September of 1930 a well southeast of Kilgore brought in 20,000 barrels daily. Following the first strike, the population of Kilgore swelled from 500 to 5,000. By 1939 Kilgore bristled with oil derricks, numbering almost 1,200 within the city limits The downtown section of Kilgore was not to be

This 1.19 acre site at the corner of Commerce and Main Streets once had 24 oil wells that produced more than 2.5 million barrels of oil. Today, 13 restored derricks stand on the site and are lighted for Christmas. (Photo courtesy Kilgore Chamber of Commerce)

spared, if "spared" is a good choice of words. The highest concentration of derricks was called "the world's richest acre." It was located at the intersection of Main and Commerce, where 24 wells produced over 2.5 million barrels of oil over 40 years of production.

The Swamp Monster of Palmetto State Park

If there really is a monster living in the swamps of the 198-acre Palmetto State Park in Gonzalez County, it can't rely on park manager Mark Rosenzweig as its publicist. Made swampy by its hot sulphur wells, which erupted into what was called "mudballs," the park is decorated by unusual tropical plants, such as dwarf palmettos, that create an eerie landscape, lending itself to apparitions such as monsters of the "Big Foot" variety. But the twelve-year veteran of the park tells us he has never actually heard of anyone seeing the so-called "Ottine monster." He did say that since the 1920s or 1930s locals have told tales of a swamp monster living in the swamps of the state park located on the San Marcos River northeast of Luling.

The "Ottine monster," as some refer to it, got its name from the almost nonexistent community of Ottine located within the park area. The community got its name by combining the name of J.A. Otto with that of his wife Christine. "I have never heard of the monster causing any mischief," Mr. Rosenzweig volunteered. He said that the nearest thing to the monster manifesting itself occurred in the 1960s or 1970s when the resident of a trailer house reported that "somebody, or something" climbed atop his trailer and shook his house.

The monster stories, he said, were often told to Boy Scouts or other groups before an impending visit into the park. "It raised the hair on the backs of their necks," he commented. The park manager stressed that there was much more to the unusual state park than the monster story. Although its swamps make a likely breeding ground for ghost stories and the like, its flora and fauna are enough to make the park an intriguing part of our state to visit.

Texas Almanac Banned in Texas Prisons

Strange as it may seem or even ludicrous, those hungering for knowledge behind the walls of Texas prisons may not include the *Texas Almanac* in their diet! According to Mary Ramos, editor of the book published by the *Dallas Morning News*, the Informations Officer for the Texas Department of Corrections advised her office that the book contains too many detailed county maps with which the prisoners could plot their escape. According to the prison representative, the *Almanac* has been banned for at least five years.

The Rugged Ranger Who Founded a California City

One of my favorite characters from out of the pages of Texas' early history is not one of the heroes of the Texas Revolution, nor is it one of the developers of the newly annexed state of Texas. He is a single, typically rugged Texas Ranger, whose heroics and bravado are the stuff the spirit of Texas is made of. Strange as it may seem, this Texas hero went on to found the city of Oakland, California.

John Coffee (Jack) Hays came to Texas from Tennessee at age nineteen. He settled in San Antonio. A surveyor by profession, he was employed by the Republic of Texas to make surveys on the Texas frontier. A noted Indian fighter, he joined the newly formed ranging company, commissioned by Sam Houston to protect the settlements around San Antonio from Comanches and other renegades ravaging the area. Hays became captain of that company of Rangers and is probably best known by Ranger aficionados for an engagement that took place in the fall of 1841, in which Hays defeated a band of about twenty-five Comanches from the summit of Enchanted Rock near Fredericksburg.

(Jack) Hays also distinguished himself in the Mexican-American War (1846-1848), where, as a colonel, he commanded the 1st Texas mounted volunteers. In 1849 during the gold rush, he led a caravan to California, where he became the first elected sheriff of San Francisco County. He served for four years.

In 1853 President Franklin Pierce appointed the former Texas Ranger surveyor general of California, where he laid out the city of Oakland. Hays amassed a considerable fortune in California. He died near Piedmont, California, April 25, 1883.

A Grand Old Lady with a Secret

Although no written documentation is available, this piece of trivia is offered because it comes directly from a descendant of the people involved. Unbelievable as it sounds, one of the most imposing man-made structures on the Gulf Coast, the once elegant Galvez Hotel on Galveston

Island, a playground for the "rich and famous," including movie stars and politicos, and which served as the summer White House for President Franklin D. Roosevelt when he vacationed on Texas' Gulf Coast, had a story of a major blunder that is still denied today by management.

Those who are supposedly in the know swear that this queen of Texas hostelries was designed with no kitchen. Those connected with its construction say that after construction bids were let, it was discovered that the plans showed no provisions for a kitchen. This hotel, where bandleader Phil Harris and Alice Fay were married, built a separate building for the kitchen. "For fire safety!" was the dodge given to cover up for this faux pas of gigantic proportions. Built in 1910-1911, this grand old lady of the Texas coast did much to breathe life into a sagging island economy.

Greer County: The County Lost to Oklahoma

On Feb. 8, 1860, legislatures for the state of Texas passed an act providing for the organizing of Greer County. With the onset of the Civil War nothing was done to establish a county government. In July of 1886 the settlers of Greer County established a government with Mangum as the county seat. A jail, two post offices, and a school system were established.

Then a boundary dispute arose between Texas and the United States as to the ownership of the county. Errors in the maps used to set the boundary led to the dispute, as well as confusion over which fork of the Red River was the proper boundary line. In 1890 President W.H. Harrison approved an act authorizing the organization of Oklahoma as a territory, and a suit against the state of Texas was filed for a final settlement of the dispute of ownership of Greer County.

The Supreme Court ruled that Greer County was subject to the jurisdiction of the United States. Although strong argument was made by Texas, which had settled the area and administered it for thirty-five years, in 1896 the Supreme Court ruled that Greer County was a part of the United States. In 1906 Greer County became a part of the state of Oklahoma.

Krin Boswell at J.R.'s Wagon Train Furniture in Ninnekah, Oklahoma, reminded us by mail that those settlers of Greer County were Texans before the court ruled their county belonged to the United States, and subsequently they became Okies, making them "Ex-Tex Okies." His letter indicated that these folks can now celebrate 100 years of "liberation from Texas." This area Texas lost to Oklahoma, "X-Tex land," is all of Oklahoma southwest of the North Fork of the Red River.

Naming the Chuck Wagon (Logic and Lore)

Taking things for granted provides little incentive for research. It is only when someone drops a contradictory bomb in your preconceived lap that it causes you to hustle off to the reference material in an effort to set the record straight about a particular matter.

Such was the case when I was alerted to the fact that my concept as to how the chuck wagon got its name might be wrong. I had always assumed that since "chuck" has been used for years as a synonym for food or grub, the name chuck wagon was a logical name for the vehicle used to

transport food on a trail drive. Then came that contradictory "bomb" that set me to hitting the books!

Recently at the National Cowboy Symposium in
Lubbock, a visitor announced to me that her grandfather
had cowboyed on the famous Charles Goodnight ranch.
She pointed out that rancher Goodnight had invented the
prototype of the chuck wagon, which cowboys and other
ranchers referred to as "Chuck's (for Charles) wagon" and
later simply as the chuck wagon. The informative lady told
us that Goodnight was fed up with delays caused by the
cook having to juggle cooking utensils and food supplies

Vittles being served up at one of the authentic chuck wagons at the
National Cowboy Symposium of 1998 in Lubbock.

each time a meal was served, as well as having to break down the small two-wheeled wagons sometimes used to transport food and utensils. So he loaded an ordinary chest of drawers into a wagon and took it to a wagon maker in a nearby town to see if it could be securely installed in the wagon so that utensils and foodstuffs could be easily managed. He also had a lid installed, which dropped down on a swinging leg to be used as a worktable for the cook.

While we found no literary reference to substantiate the chest of drawers theory or the use of the nickname "Chuck" being a part of the naming of the wagon, we found ample evidence of Mr. Goodnight's role in the development of this vital wagon used in trail drives in Texas and the Southwest! In the biography of Charles Goodnight, entitled *Charles Goodnight, Cowman and Plainsman* by J. Evetts Haley, the researcher wrote, "He bought the gear of a government wagon, pulled it over to a woodworker in Parker County and had it entirely rebuilt with the toughest wood available, seasoned bois d'arc. Its axles were of iron instead of the usual wood, and in place of a tar bucket, he put in a can of tallow to be used in greasing.

"For the back end of the wagon he built the first chuck box he had ever seen, and recalled that it had been changed very little to this day. Its hinged lid let down on a swinging leg for a cook's table."

Jon E. Lewis wrote in *The Mammoth Book of the West:* "Invented by Charles Goodnight, the chuck wagon was an adapted Conestoga, made of Osage orange (bois d'arc), the toughest wood Goodnight knew of, the wood Indians used for their bows." Hence the French name bois d'arc or wood of the bow.

In the book *The Cowboys,* Time-Life Books, William H. Forbis wrote, in speaking of the chuck wagon, "Credit for the ultimate design of the wagon belongs to cattle baron Charles Goodnight, who in 1866 rebuilt for his trail crew a surplus Army wagon, picked primarily for its extra-durable iron axles. To the basic wagon bed, where bulk goods such as foodstuffs and bedrolls were to be stored, Goodnight added the already customary trail-drive appendages. But the innovation that made the Goodnight wagon unique at the time, and a useful prototype for all self-respecting wagons that followed, was the design and installation of a chuck box. Perched at the rear of the wagon, facing aft, it had a hinged lid that let down on a swinging leg to form a worktable."

Rommel's Afrika Korp Occupied Part of Texas

At one time members of the elite and infamous Nazi fighting force known as the Afrika Korp occupied part of Texas, just not in the way their highly decorated general or his exalted fuhrer thought they would. It was not the general's fighting prowess that allowed his elite Korp to occupy a small portion of Central Texas, but rather the superior military strength and tenacity of the American and British military that resulted in thousands of his troops being among the first prisoners of war to be incarcerated in Camp Hearne in Central Texas.

During WW II the great number of German prisoners captured brought much pressure on the U.S. to build more and more POW camps. In March of 1942 the Chamber of Commerce of Hearne, Texas, set in motion a move to have a POW camp built in their region, believing it would be a boon to their economy.

Namesakes Remembered

There are at least three of Texas' 254 counties that have county seats which, when combined with the county name, give the name of the person for whom the county was named. They are Gail, county seat of Borden; Anson, county seat of Jones County; and McKinney, county seat of Collin County. Gail Borden was an early publisher and inventor. Anson Jones was the last president of the Republic of Texas. Collin McKinney was an early settler.

Texas State Mammal Has Strange Reproduction

The nine-banded armadillo, named Texas' state small mammal by the legislature, has a most unusual reproduction pattern. Each birth produces a litter of four, all of the same sex.

"Christ The King" Watches Over Texas

The Sierra de Cristo Rey (Christ the King) is topped by a 40-foot statue of the crucifixion of Christ.

The author and a nine-banded armadillo. Normally fleet of foot, this one failed to outrun the taxidermist.

Although it is in New Mexico, it overlooks one of Texas' largest cities, El Paso.

Underwater Travel in Texas

One section of a major road system in Texas is under-water 24 hours a day, 365 days a year yet is traversed by thousands of cars and trucks daily. It is Harris County's Washburn Tunnel built in 1950. This important part of the Harris County road system goes under the Houston Ship Channel between Galena Park and the city of Pasadena. Newcomers to Houston, where daily rain is not uncommon, are sometimes startled to hear radio reporters make the tongue-in-cheek observation, "The Washburn Tunnel is underwater this morning."

Lufkin: Founded on Lore or Logs?

In writing about our state we have always expressed our feelings of respect for the salt-of-the-earth folks of East Texas. On at least one occasion, in an attempt to paint a word picture of that marvelous green belt of Texas and the folks who call it home, we have indicated that there is about as much lore and legend in that part of Texas as there are loblolly pines. East Texans have demonstrated a pen-chant for passing on colorful stories from one generation to another to tell the region's history and culture. Some of them are pure conjecture, perhaps based on a grain of fact; others are an altered version of the facts that got slightly exaggerated or out of square with the truth in the process of the retelling! A few of these slightly embellished stories have found their way into "factual" historical accounts, which often makes it difficult for the researcher to separate fact from legend. One of these questionable East Texas tales is the basis for this item of trivia.

Although disputable, if one knows the character of the folks who have East Texas roots and factors in the time in history of the alleged incident, the story becomes more feasible. We are grateful to Mr. Bob Bowman of Lufkin, a recognized historian of Angelina County, of which Lufkin is county seat, for sharing with us his copy of a history of Lufkin, *The Lufkin That Was*, written in 1982, the centennial of that city. From it we have drawn many historical facts. His knowledge of that city's heritage is admirable. One example told by East Texans is how the city of Lufkin was founded.

Angelina County's greatest natural resource is its literal sea of pine forests, which was virtually impossible to take advantage of because of the inability to transport any fallen trees to sawmills. Most shipping of goods in the late 1800s was done by wagon and teams of oxen. Area rivers were not suitable to float logs to sawmills. Wagon shipping was slow and tedious in the sparsely settled land. The year of Lufkin's founding, 1882, signaled the beginning of an era which brought the railroad and, as a result, the first timber boom to East Texas. Meeting this opportunity head-on was Paul Bremond, successful Houston merchant and president of the Houston and Texas Central Railroad. Bremond decided to build the Houston East and West Texas Railroad. It is out of the construction of the HE&WT railroad that the questionable lore of the founding of Lufkin comes to us.

At the time of the construction of the HE&WT the county seat and business center of Angelina County was Homer. "At that time," writes Mr. Bowman, "Lufkin was little more than a few homes strung out on a dirt road in a forest clearing. Then into Angelina County came a surveying crew from Paul Bremond's HE&WT Railroad to plot the route for the railroad's push through East Texas."

The crew supposedly began its work by surveying a route that would take the railroad through Homer, the county seat. The told and retold story goes that the surveying crew decided to spend Saturday night in the saloons of Homer. As the night wore on, their "letting off steam" became a bit too rowdy. Constable W.B. "Buck" Green put the rambunctious crew in the local hoosegow. The next morning the men paid their fines and were freed. The constable's action so infuriated the chief of the survey crew, identified as Captain Edwin P. Lufkin, that, according to lore, he ordered the crew to plot a new route for the railroad which would bypass Homer and run the line in the proximity of what was known then as Denman Springs.

Whether or not the brawl at Homer caused the rerouting of the railroad is debatable; however, the story is vouched for by some of the county's oldest residents. Regardless of the cause, the action turned Homer into a ghost town. Soon town sites were being offered at the new terminus of the railroad, and businesses were being built. It wasn't until the railroad arrived and the depot was built on property donated by Colonel Lafayette Denman, that Lufkin began to develop around the depot.

Even the naming of the town is in dispute, nothing new for East Texans! Some insist the town was named for Edwin P. Lufkin, chief of the surveying crew. Others are of the belief that the town was named for Abraham P. Lufkin of Galveston, a close friend of railroad president Paul Bremond.

Bean's "Hanging Judge" Image Invalid

According to personnel at the Judge Roy Bean visitor's center in Langtry, Texas, Judge Bean's reputation as a "hanging judge" was invalid. As only a justice of the peace, Bean had no authority to hang anyone or sentence anyone to hang.

Famed Texas judge Roy Bean holds court for two accused horse thieves at his Jersey Lilly Saloon and courtroom in Langtry, Texas.

Fort Worth "Where the West Begins"

The city of Fort Worth's slogan, "Where the West begins," has no basis in any modern map markings. Those Texas cities located east of Fort Worth have come to think of that city as the demarcation line indicating the beginning of West Texas. The much-publicized slogan originated as the result of an Indian treaty. On September 29, 1843, General Edward H. Tarrant, for whom Tarrant County is named, and General George W. Terrell met with leaders of nine Indian tribes and signed the Bird's Fort Treaty, calling for Indians to end conflicts and establishing a line separating Indian lands from territory open for colonization. The Indians were not to enter lands west of that line, which was drawn through what is today Fort Worth. From this, Fort Worth adopted the slogan "Where the West begins." The city's cattle and cowboy culture lends credence to this descriptive slogan.

Shelby County's "Trap Door to Safety"

If we are to believe the Hollywood version of the Old West and the pulp fiction dime novels written about the lives and times of early Texas, the very mention of the words "trap door" struck fear in the hearts of those whose activities skirted the law, particularly those who participated in the outrageous crime of cattle rustling. To those

miscreants of early Texas the words "trap door" conjured up the ghastly image of their standing on a gallows with a hangman's noose around their neck, as they awaited the fatal plunge that would pay their debt to society for their errant ways.

The Shelby County courthouse in Center, Texas, has a built-in trap door that once served as a safety feature, rather than something to be feared. In a conversation with county judge Floyd A. "Dock" Watson, we were told that when the 1885 county courthouse was built, a trap door was installed near the judge's bench to provide the presiding judge a handy means of escape from irate defendants. The door provided access by way of stairs to the judge's chambers below the bench.

The judge told us that, while there are surely stories of such escapes, he knows of no such incidences personally. Although the trap door had been sealed off for some time, the judge had it reopened, as it was such an interesting attraction in the county courthouse. Judge Watson said he especially enjoyed leading school children on tours. One can understand how this attraction of days gone by would pique the imagination of a child of school age!

Romance of the Road Not So Easy for Early Texas Motorists

While the advent of the motor car made travel in Texas easier and faster, finding one's way didn't come easier until later. Today when the urge to hit the road or necessity puts us behind the wheel on Texas highways and byways, most of us rely on memory of previous trips to navigate our cars to our destination. If any doubts arise before or during our journey, all we have to do is pull into the nearest service station, whatever the breed, and ask for a Texas road map. Generally, as has been the case since the early part of the twentieth century when oil companies did everything they could to stimulate road travel, a free road map will be provided to the motorist. This has not always been the case!

At first Texas roads had no names or numbers. Motorists used detailed road logs that described every bend and turn in the road, including streams that were fordable. Sometimes these logbooks were a hundred pages or more. Not very practical, particularly if one traveled numerous regions. These log books disappeared as roads were marked with colors and numbers.

Before there were interstates, some of Texas' national routes had names like "The Bankhead Highway" that ran from Texarkana through Dallas, Abilene, Midland, to El Paso. Other famous names were "Dixie Highway" and "The Old Spanish Trail." In the mid-1920s state highway officials began to establish rudiments of our numbered highway system. This led to the road maps that we use on most of the Texas highway trips we take today. The romantic-sounding names of the routes may be gone, but the details of modern Texas road maps make travel in Texas more convenient and comfortable.

Texas' "Bat-Cave" Jail

Although it was never inhabited by bats, the dungeon-like jail of Fort Davis, Texas, was so called because it was located beneath the old adobe county courthouse in Fort Davis, the one-time county seat of Presidio County. The jail's entrance was a trap door and ladder in the floor of the sheriff's office. This arrangement did much to discourage jailbreaks from the foreboding place of incarceration. Minutes of the county commissioner's court tell us that the jail was furnished with five iron cages and a scaffold. This must have added to the jail's reputation as being dungeon-like. The old "Bat-cave" courthouse was replaced in 1911 by a modern concrete and stone structure.

Jimplecute, East Texas' "Frightening Dragon"

In Fred Tarpley's book *Jefferson, Riverport to the Southwest*, the author provides interesting insight into one of Texas' perplexing enigmas. One of the state's most historically rich towns is the East Texas town of Jefferson, which, although not located on the Gulf coast, became one of Texas' major shipping ports. But that is a story within itself.

One of the town's earliest newspapers had a puzzling name that generated much speculation as to its origin and its meaning. Mr. Tarpley writes, "The earliest known newspaper in Jefferson was the *Jefferson Democrat* published in 1847." He goes on to explain that on Dec. 8, 1848, a prospectus was published for the *JIMPLECUTE* announcing it would begin publication. The author tells us that the newspaper with the confounding name bore a masthead, which included a line drawing of a mythical creature: "a crouched animal with the mouth of a dragon, the head with the full headdress of an Indian, the body of a large armadillo, the front legs and feet like those of a lion ready to spring." The editor said that the drawing came from a painting done by a tramp painter who said that he knew what a jimplecute looked like and agreed to paint a sign for the newspaper.

Jimplecute's masthead with the forked-tail creature, as could be expected, drew much discussion as to the meaning of the name and the animal it displayed. While the drawing had previously been used on publications to frighten super-stitious slaves before and during the Civil War, the newspaper's name was, according to Mr. Tarpley's book, an acronym which laid out the town's motto: "Join Industry, Manufacturing, Planting, Labor, Energy, Capital, (in) Unity Together, Everlastingly." The name was evidently supposed to advocate friendship and unity between every interest in Jefferson.

Tarpley tells us, "From 1925 until 1937, the name was discarded in Jefferson and the newspaper published as the *Jefferson Journal*. The intended meaning of the Jimplecute may never be known," says the author, "since the original publisher left no surviving comment on the name."

Cougars on the Colorado!

Although the so-called "Wild and Woolly West" is no more, I beg my readers to indulge me this brief autobio-graphical sketch to tell of a segment of Texas wildness that did not disappear with the vast herds of buffalo and legend-ary longhorn cattle.

Although well known to old-timers living along the Col-orado River, the tawny cougars that prowl its valley communities and bordering mountains are not so well known by other Texans. As a child growing up in the 1930s and '40s, the coming of summer signaled, among other things, our family's annual trek to the Mills County com-munity of Big Valley on the wide and muddy Colorado River that knifed through the county past my mother's birthplace. As a city-dwelling youth, nearly everything

Another menace to Mills County livestock was the jaguar. Called the most powerful and dangerous of the big cats in the Americas, jaguars were known to roam from the Southwestern U.S. to the tropics of South America. The last jaguar killed in Mills County was by Homer Brown, Henry Morris, and John Walton, in 1903. This photo shows Homer Brown and Henry Morris examining the jaguar they shot during a hunt with experienced hunting hounds. One of Brown's hounds, a red bone Beagle named Jack, was killed by the big cat during the hunt. (Photo courtesy of Glynn Collier of Goldthwaite, Texas)

there was an adventure. Above all, one thing captured my youthful imagination. It was the stuff legends are made of. It was cougar talk!

Each year one of my Mills County relatives would begin a discussion of the most recent cougar scares. Called by various names, such as "mountain lions, pumas, panthers, or just 'the big cats'," the name most often used by locals and the name which conjured up the most hair-raising image, at least among us young folks, was "cougar." Hardly a reunion passed without someone in Big Valley reinforcing the stories of the big cats with the long slinky bodies and even longer tails, preying on livestock in the area along the Colorado. Sightings or sounds of the big cat, spoken of as if it were only one animal, were discussed by adults in quiet details, while we youngsters listened, fascinated and somewhat in fear. One aunt related how a member of her family, alerted by the bawling of a calf, went to the cow pen behind her house and "There he sat!" At the sight or scent of her, the big cat tensed his tawny body and sprang gracefully over a shoulder-high fence and fled into a stand of nearby trees. Another neighbor reported hearing the cry that, as he put it, "sounded like the scream of a woman. It had to have been one of the Colorado's cougars," he allowed. Another family member, while looking for cows in a pasture, saw two "yearling" cougar cubs stretched out in peaceful sleep on a farm implement. He said he didn't wait around to see if their parents were in the neighborhood.

All of these stories came to life one summer when one of the men folk at the reunion found indisputable proof that a cougar had made a recent visit to my grandfather's place. In the sandy lane that separated my grandfather's place from a field, a large carp was found. It had obviously been brought up from the Colorado about a mile away. Distinctive claw marks gave evidence to its being pulled apart to be eaten. Additional paw prints of the cougar were measured in an attempt to estimate its size. The sand had recorded his nocturnal visit.

That night few of us kids slept on the large wrap-around porch on which quilts and cots were placed so we kids could free up bed space for the reunion's overflow crowd of adults. But the cougar's appearance not more than fifty feet away had driven us inside to sleep on the floor.

My research into these big cats, after I became an adult, revealed that the cougars of the Colorado in Mills County had, in all likelihood, been Mexican mountain lions who had crossed into Texas and followed the mountain ranges north to enlarge their territories for hunting prey. Not all of them returned to their homeland, as there is still "cougar talk" in Mills County now and then.

"Father of Texas" Legally Changed Name

The man whose name is, perhaps, most closely associated with Texas and who, by bringing the first colonists into Texas, earned the title "Father of Texas," Stephen F. Austin, legally changed his first name to Estavan, Spanish for Stephen. While in Mexico for a year on colonization business, Austin became a Mexican citizen. He learned to read and write Spanish fluently and earned the confidence of Mexican officials. He was known there by the name Estavan. Brian Butcher, historian at the San Jacinto Museum, advises that when Austin became a Mexican citizen, as was required of all settlers in Texas, he then legally changed his name to the Mexican spelling. Perhaps as much to please the Mexicans, as to meet any legal requirements.

Already being known by the Spanish name made this a natural move.

General Pablo Houston, Hero of San Jacinto!

The name just doesn't roll off the Texas tongue like Sam Houston! And yet, strange as it might sound, the revered Texas hero once officially used the name "Sam Pablo Houston." The new *Handbook of Texas* informs us that in 1837 Houston filed for divorce from his first wife, Eliza, who had abandoned the marriage after only a few weeks. As prescribed by Mexican law, Houston was then baptized into the Catholic Church under the name Samuel Pablo Houston. Why the legendary hero chose Pablo as the required second name is not known. One can only speculate that, as in the case of Stephen F. Austin, who changed his first name to the Mexican spelling, it would enhance his standing with the Mexican authorities. This is, however, pure speculation!

Santa Anna's "Battlefield Wedding"; Where Was the General When the Alamo Fell?

Although apocryphal in nature, an often repeated and intriguing story has trickled down through the pages of Alamo history. It is the story of Mexican general Santa Anna's overactive libido and how it may have served as an ally to the Texians in their fight for independence. While many are familiar with the story of the mulatto servant Emily Morgan, said to have been the model for the saga and song "Yellow Rose of Texas," who kept the general occupied at the battle of San Jacinto, far fewer are aware of the "Napoleon of the West's" battlefield wedding at the battle of the Alamo.

According to events surrounding the general's life, it is reported that this bit of debauchery on the part of the Mexican leader may well have diverted his attention during the siege of the Alamo. Although the outcome was not affected, the circumstances of his dalliance could have been crucial.

True to his reputation as a womanizer, Santa Anna's attention was distracted by amorous activities. Although the general had a wife in Mexico and although the battle for the Alamo was underway, he diverted his attention toward Melchora Berrera, the beautiful seventeen-year-old daughter of a prominent San Antonio widow. This was not uncommon for the general, who was known to keep company with several mistresses, some of whom accompanied him on his campaigns. Desiring to meet Melchora, Santa Anna asked General Manuel Castrillon to bring her to his quarters. The story is that Castrillon refused to act as his procurer. Later Santa Anna was able to get an introduction by someone else.

But Senora Berrera refused to let him see her daughter unless he married her. To fool Melchora's mother, the general arranged for one of his sergeants, an actor, to disguise himself as a priest and perform a mock wedding. The general was enjoying his "honeymoon" when the Alamo fell to the Mexican army.

Why the Lone Ranger Wears a Mask

If you grew up listening to and later watching the adventures of the "Lone Ranger" and have wondered why this defender of the rights of men and fighter for justice wears a mask, this trivia item is for you! Yes, this peculiar trait of a fictional character has enough of a Texas connection to fit snugly into our items of Texas trivia.

While our collection of Texas trivia is based on fact and well-known lore, this fragment torn from a fertile imagination has, as its basis, one of Texas' beloved icons, the Texas Rangers. Thus it warrants, we believe, special consideration and inclusion.

According to reference material enlightening us on early radio shows, in 1930 George Trindel, while searching for a radio script he could submit as a possible radio show about the Old West, invented a character based on the Texas Rangers by the name of John Reid. One of the early story lines finds Ranger Reid and his troop of five Rangers, one of which was his brother, engaged in a blazing gun-battle with the Butch Cavandish gang. The reference tells us that all the Rangers were killed save Reid, who was wounded. The lone remaining Ranger told his Indian friend Tonto, who had nursed him back to health, "If this evil gang realizes that one Ranger survived, they would hunt him down and kill him." To this Tonto replied, "Them no think you survive, me bury five dead rangers, but make six graves."

Reid has now become the "Lone Ranger." Reid realizes the Cavandishes know him by sight and he will always be in danger. He tells Tonto that he must create a disguise or wear a mask. "Yes, that's it, I'll wear a mask." Reference material tells us that Texas Ranger Reid, now the Lone Ranger, sought out the body of his brother, who was a member of his troop, and cut a strip off his brother's black leather vest, from which he fashioned the familiar mask. Trindel's story of the Lone Ranger and his secret, although fiction, further enhances our image of the individuals selected to make up this elite arm of our Texas criminal justice system.

1897 UFO Crash, Alien Burial, Cannot Withstand Scrutiny!

Six years before the Wright Brothers' Kitty Hawk flight and decades before man's conquest of space and the advent of "Star Wars," a newspaper story with the dateline "Aurora, Texas" started a feeding frenzy of reporters and curious visitors. Years later this escalated into a rush of

What happened in Aurora in 1897?

Cigar-shaped spaceship allegedly crashed in town

By JIM MARRS
Star-Telegram Writer

Many years ago, some residents of Aurora apparently felt they had a Close Encounter of the Third Kind, even before Columbia Pictures did.

Columbia debuted the movie, "Close Encounters of the Third Kind," Wednesday, but Aurora's near encounter of the weird kind was April 17, 1897.

What really happened in Aurora? The honest-to-Gospel truth is that no one can say for sure.

First, there was the news story printed in the old Fort Worth Register a day or so later. The story said an airship sailed over Aurora, collided with a windmill and crashed.

In the wreckage, according to the news account, was the disfigured body of the pilot. Enough of the body remained to "show that he was not an inhabitant of this world."

People came from all around to view the wreckage, the story said. Many gathered up pieces of the "strange metal" as souvenirs. The ship's pilot reportedly was buried in the cemetery in Aurora, a tiny town on Texas 114 between Rhome and Boyd in Wise County.

THE STORY, plus or minus some embellishments, has cropped up now and again since then.

Today, the handful of Aurora residents are about equally divided on whether there is any truth to the story.

Etta Pegues, a newspaper correspondent for Aurora, steadfastly maintains the whole thing was a hoax dreamed up by S.E. Hayden, an Aurora cotton buyer. However,

her beliefs stem primarily from talks with an elderly woman who, as a child, lived near Aurora at the time of the supposed crash.

Mrs. Pegues said the woman recalled that day because someone came by their house and told her father about the crash. Her father, who she said never went to the crash site, simply laughed and said it was probably a joke being played by Hayden.

• • •

OTHER EYEWITNESSES gave a different story. C.C. Stephens in 1973 told a Dallas newspaper he was working with his father that day and saw a bright, cigar-shaped object glide overhead. Stephens said there was an explosion and a fire which lit up the sky.

"The next day, my father rode a horse into Aurora to look at the scene and said it looked like a mass of torn metal and burned rubble," Stephens said. He added that his father said nothing about the pilot.

"Of course, he didn't get to the site until the next day, and by that time, if there were some crewmen they would have been buried," he said.

Also in 1973, several newsmen, including a Star-Telegram reporter, visited the Aurora Cemetery and did, in fact, locate a small, unmarked grave which was identified as that of the ship's pilot.

• • •

BILL CASE, aviation writer for the Dallas Times Herald, went over the grave with a metal detector and discovered there were several bits of metal in the grave.

In addition, the remnants of an old tombstone on the grave had the

PUZZLED
...Aurora searcher

carving of part of a saucer-shaped object on it. The intriguing headstone was stolen soon after news stories were printed.

Talk began about exhuming the grave, but irate Aurora residents went to a local peace justice, who issued a restraining order prohibiting anyone from digging in the cemetery.

There matters rested until sever-

al months later when Case and a member of the Midwest Unidentified Flying Object Network again visited Aurora.

Case pulled his metal detector from his car to show his companion the metal readings at the grave site — and was shocked to find no readings.

He later said, upon close inspection of the grave, he discovered three small holes bored into the ground.

"Someone with some very sophisticated equipment apparently came along, located the metal in the grave and extracted it," Case said. "It would be interesting to know who."

Case died in December 1974.

• • •

TODAY, THE grave's headstone is still missing, the metal is gone from the grave and bits of metal recovered at the crash site have caused mixed reactions from scientists who have studied them.

Some scientists in Oklahoma said their analysis of the metal showed nothing unusual. But a physicist at North Texas State University in Denton examined some of the metal and found at least one piece "puzzling."

He said the metal appeared to be some type of fused aluminum and added that if that bit of metal was from the 1897 period, it would present a very puzzling problem. No one had developed such metal at that time.

So there things stand. And the question remains.

What really happened in Aurora that morning of April 17, 1897?

UFO nuts, who still present a problem for locals, according to a letter from Rosalie Gregg, chairperson of the Wise County Historical Commission. She asked us not to portray the much-publicized event as being true in our book.

From all the newspaper clippings, which date from 1968 through the 1970s, we have assembled a fairly accurate description of the reported events that kicked off the early UFO craze in North Texas. *Dallas Morning News* columnist Frank Tolbert said a story in his paper's April 19, 1897 edition reported, "About 6 o'clock this morning early risers of Aurora were astonished at the sudden appearance of the airship which has been sailing through the country." (There had, at the time, been numerous reports of "mysterious airships," mostly reported in America's Midwest).

Tolbert continues, "A reporter with the by-line of Hayden reported that a spaceship had crashed in Aurora and the pilot was to be buried in the local cemetery." The news story continued: "It (the airship) sailed directly over the public square, and when it reached the north end of town it collided with Judge Proctor's windmill and went to pieces with a terrible explosion, scattering pieces over several acres of ground, wrecking the judge's windmill, and destroying his flower garden.

"The pilot of the ship is supposed to be the only one aboard, and while his remains are badly disfigured, enough of his remains has been picked up to show he was not an inhabitant of this world. The pilot's funeral will take place today." (Author's note: One newspaper account credited the pilot's alien origin to a citizen, T. J. Weems, who is identified as a "U.S. Signal Service officer and astronomy authority").

A headstone placed on the "alien's" grave had part of a carving of a saucer-shaped object on it. The stone was stolen soon after the news broke.

Close scrutiny shoots holes in spaceship story. The spaceship story made out of whole cloth began to unravel under close scrutiny! For one thing, reporter Hayden turned out to be a cotton broker. And T.J. Weems, the "astronomy authority," was a local blacksmith. Newspaper accounts said that justice of the peace Judge Proctor had no windmill.

Perhaps the most damning of all the detractors of the story is the affidavit of Mrs. Robbie Hanson of El Paso, Texas, who called the story a joke. Mrs. Hanson was born in Aurora in 1885 and said she was twelve years old when the traveler's craft was supposed to have crashed.

"I was in school that day and it just never happened," she flatly stated. In her affidavit Mrs. Hanson said "My father was the town constable and he would have to be one of the first to know if such a thing happened." Mrs. Hanson said the story was contrived by Judge Proctor, who printed a one-page weekly newspaper. In her affidavit Mrs. Hanson said Judge Proctor was known to regularly print such far-fetched tales in his paper as a joke. This personal affidavit, along with the other known misrepresentations, shoots down this excitement-generating story.

This hoax, inferred some newspaper articles, was concocted mainly to generate an interest in this small community, which, said one article, was "dying-on-the-vine." One clipping quoted a local as saying that at the time, "Not even a Martian would be caught dead in Aurora!" Regardless of motive, the spaceship crash was truly a Texas-size hoax!

Did Jesse James Choose Texas in Which to Die?

Those knowledgeable in the lives and deaths of the infamous outlaws of the nineteenth century will tell you that Jesse James was shot to death by the man immortalized in song as, "That dirty little coward" Robert Ford, in his home in Missouri in 1882. The train robber and murderer of legend and lore (considered by many a folk hero, "robbing from the rich and giving to the poor") wasn't permitted to rest in peace in his Missouri soil. Folks in Granbury, Texas, pop. 5,000 contend that James feigned death and wandered south to their town where he lived out of the limelight as J.W. Gates. Their contentions were solidified when, following his death in 1951, a grave marker was erected that read, "Jesse Woodson James, September 5, 1847—August 15, 1951, Supposedly killed in 1882." The marker bore Jesse's true name.

The fact that this identity would have made the deceased 104 years old didn't phase those who contended that Gates was really Jesse James. This comes, incidentally, from the same Texas town that claimed that another of its residents, John St. Helen, a Shakespeare-spouting saloonkeeper, was actually John Wilkes Booth, the actor accused of assassinating President Abraham Lincoln. One is forced to ponder why so many infamous characters of history chose this small town in the rolling hills of Texas to live out their final days.

First Texas Cavalry of the U.S. (The Texas Military Unit That Fought for the Union in the Civil War)

Although it is a well-known fact that, although Texas was a Confederate state during the Civil War, many individual Texans served in the Union army. What is not so well known is that one Texas military unit fought for the Union forces. The First Texas Cavalry of the U.S. was a regiment organized and commanded by Edmund J. Davis, later to be governor of Texas. This Texas Cavalry unit fought mainly in the Rio Grand Valley, Louisiana, and Mississippi.

Japanese Partially Responsible for Dallas Flying Red Horse Landmark

Strange as it may seem, Japanese tradition is partially responsible for Dallas' famed Flying Red Horse landmark. In truth, the petroleum company's trademark, which was

1911–After the breakup of the Standard Oil Trust, the newly independent Vacuum Oil Company registers a white image of Pegasus as a trademark for its leading grade of gasoline in Cape Town, South Africa.

placed atop the Magnolia Building in 1934 in honor of the National Petroleum Association convention to be held in Dallas, was not always red.

The story of Pegasus, the official name of the famous trademark, begins shortly after the organization of Socony Vacuum in 1931. At that time the oil company, which was to become Mobil Oil Company, adopted Pegasus as a trademark. A history of the trademark provided by Mobil informs us that in 1911, "After the breakup of the Standard Oil Trust, the newly independent Vacuum Oil Company registered a white image of Pegasus as the trademark of its leading grade of gasoline in Cape Town, South Africa. Meanwhile, the Standard Oil Company of New York (Socony) used a red Pegasus to promote its fuel in Japan and Indonesia."

The history goes on to reveal the fact that it was Mobil Sekiyu in Japan, however, that first colored it red. A recent Dallas newspaper article explains, "Mobil was forced to change its color from white to red after discovering that a white horse symbolized death in Japan." Although the "symbol of death" tradition is not specifically referred to, company history does credit the horse's red color to the Japanese. Had it not been for this Japanese tradition, perhaps Dallas would have as its best-known landmark the Flying White Horse?

Shackelford County's "Alphabet Jail"

Albany, Texas, county seat of Shackelford County, is the home of a Texas county jail with two special attractions to visitors. Not to those sent there by judicial decree, but to those of us who ferret out unique Texas attractions. According to historical records, verified by jail historian Diana

Nail, outlaw and occasional lawman John Selman escaped from the jail in the late 1970s. Selman found his way to El Paso where he earned a notch on his gun as well as a special place in Texas history. He is given credit as being the gunslinger who killed badman turned lawyer John Wesley Hardin.

The Albany jail has, it should be noted, one additional claim to fame. It was given the name "Alphabet Jail." It was so named because when it was built in 1878, the county suffered from a lack of funds and the stone masons carved their initials into each stone they cut to be insured they would be paid for their work. Ms. Nail advised us that the initials can be seen today both inside and outside the jail. This example of piecework payment, strange as it is, is true!

"But Only God Can Make a Tree!" and the Champions Are Found in Texas

The New Jersey-born poet Joyce Kilmer humbly ended his internationally famous poem "Trees" by giving the Almighty credit for creating the most majestic of all his earthly plants. Had the poet not been killed in the battle of the Marne in the First World War, he might have later been inspired to write how Texas had been chosen to produce many of the most majestic of these, His leafy creations. The Texas Big Tree Registry of the Texas Forest Service lists over two hundred state champion and co-champion trees. Those having a preconceived picture of Texas as being only plains and desert have not been privileged to see these trees. Like so many of the state's claims of a grandiose nature, as Larry Hodge so aptly put it in his marvelous *Texas Highways* story on Texas trees, "Texas is not just a state of trees, but a state of BIG trees!"

The following examples are offered as proof to skeptics: Our state tree, the pecan, is, appropriately, one of our national champions. This giant is located in Weatherford. The privately owned giant stands as tall as a twelve-story building. Its massive branches spread 159 feet. Its girth requires four people to reach around it. Scientists have estimated its age at 1,100 years old. Further west near Fort Davis one can find the national champion Rio Grande cottonwood tree, requiring no less than six people to reach around it. The state champion coastal live oak tree grows near Rockport. Having a circumference of 422 inches, this Texas champion boasts the largest girth of any tree in the Big Tree Registry! According to the *1998-99 Texas Almanac* this tree, known as "Big Tree," is estimated to be more than 1,000 years old. Some of these Texas giants sport a growth of Spanish moss hanging from their leafy boughs, which gives the impression of their having long gray beards as testimony to their being the patriarchs of Texas trees.

I am indebted to Larry Hodge of Mason for his permission to use excerpts from his story "Texas Champion Trees" in the January 1999 issue of *Texas Highways* magazine in this entry, as well as the assistance of the Texas Forest Service, which provided much information of value.

Dallas County's Most Whizzed-By Cemetery

Usually when we think of someone being laid to their eternal rest, we think of their final resting place as a pastoral scene interrupted only by the assorted headstones which mark the additional resting places of those interred there. We of the twentieth century have come to expect, if not totally accept, a smattering of plastic floral offerings atop some of the graves. While some of the monuments honoring the deceased may be more elaborate than others, as a general rule they all reflect the love and respect intended to be shown to the person at rest! In some of the larger, more urban cemeteries a wisp of music may be heard wafting through the air. What we have come to expect of our final resting place is, above all, an atmosphere of quiet,

Texas' most "whizzed-by" cemetery can be found in Irving, Texas, in a small strip of land between the eastbound lanes of Highway 183 and the service road. It includes a small strand of trees. (Photo by Marianne Cannon)

respectful repose. This is, no doubt, why our rural cemeteries seem so quietly restful. Most rural cemeteries originate either as a family's private burial ground, selected by the patriarch or matriarch of the family whose wish it is to be laid to rest in a place known to them for its peaceful surroundings, or in connection with a church in the community to serve its parishioners. An example of the latter is the 140-year-old Denton County cemetery adjacent to the Presbyterian church in Flower Mound, which we wrote of previously. All of this leads to an example of the former, which, unexpectedly, is a much-inquired-about Dallas County cemetery.

Of the many cemeteries we have visited gathering facts for our trivia collection, one of the most interesting examples of family burial plots is a bit too dangerous to explore! Its dangers are not the type generated by superstitious minds or local lore that would have us believe that the graveyard is inhabited by saints, spooks, and the like. No! We are speaking of a burial ground that has been seen and wondered about by hundreds of our readers as they departed the south exit of the DFW airport traveling in the direction of Irving and Dallas. It is an example of a family burial ground located in a few trees in the median strip between the eastbound and westbound lanes of Airport Freeway, otherwise known as Highway 183.

Only a mile or so from the airport exit, it contains less than twenty-five graves. Its uniqueness is not only its proximity to one of America's busiest aviation hubs, but also its size. How many cemeteries do you know that are small enough to fit into a highway median? This explains the inherent dangers we spoke of in exploring this pygmaean cemetery. They are not the threat from the "world beyond" or such spiritual phenomenon; they are very tangible and understood by us all. Anyone who has traveled this main artery knows the difficulty one would have finding a place to park and cross the traffic lanes to explore this burial place. What once was a pastoral place of peace is now whizzed by at speeds ranging from the allowed 55 miles per hour, to speeds in the hundreds of miles an hour generated by airplanes landing and taking off. All unheard of at the time of the cemetery's founding.

In order to understand why this place was selected as someone's final resting place, one has to turn back the pages of Dallas County history. The Irving Public Library tells us that the cemetery is the Thompkins family cemetery and is located on the Thompkins family farm purchased by Isaac C. Thompkins in 1865. The library further informs us that Thompkins expressed a desire to be buried on the farm. Upon his death in 1897, his wife selected a peaceful spot by a small grove of trees for his burial site. This is the place we see near the airport exit. We were told that highway engineers routed Highway 183 to accommodate the burial ground. It is our understanding that there is still one member of the Thompkins family who has expressed a desire to be buried in this far-from-peaceful cemetery.

Although Mr. Thompkins' final resting place is far from the peaceful, pastoral setting he envisioned, it has been seen by thousands over the past decades, making him somewhat of a celebrity, but making the standard inscription "RIP" ludicrous.

Part V

History Revisited

*I*t is human nature to pause briefly when we see a mirror and take a quick and perhaps self-conscious peek to see how we appear to others at the moment. History is nothing more than a looking glass reflecting our past. While, as in our appearance, some things in our history seem more obvious than others do, there are uncountable instances that tend to go unnoticed unless pointed out to us. These minor incidences reflect a vital segment of our whole history. Texas history is no different! Certain things, like the Alamo, rise like cream to the top of our memories when the word history is mentioned.

But what about the "Sunday houses" of some early Texas settlers, or the "Jackass mail?" These are just a few of the more trivial reflections to be seen in the mirror of Texas history that go untaught in public schools. And that is exactly what trivia is all about! These and other similar events are captured in this section of this second edition of *A Treasury of Texas Trivia.*

The Day Santa Claus Was Lynched

Bold Headlines in the *Cisco Daily News,* December 23, 1927 edition, scream the news that was to lead to the lynching of Santa Claus on November 18, 1929. The mild-mannered West Texas town hardly needed the big black headlines to remind them of the day's tragic events! Most of its citizenry, many of which were in town shopping for the Christmas that was just hours away, had heard the shots that punctuated the Christmas atmosphere when a small group of bank robbers led by a pistol-packing Marshall Ratliff, dressed in a Santa Claus suit to prevent suspicion, robbed the First National Bank of Cisco. They left a trail of blood, some their own, mingled with that of nine Cisco citizens including several of the city's lawmen, in their wake.

Their trials resulted in hefty prison sentences for several of the robbers and death sentences for others, including the Santa Claus bank robber. Feigning insanity while awaiting his ride on "Old Sparky"(the convict's term for the electric chair), Marshall Ratliff was, minus his Santa Claus suit, returned to Eastland County for a sanity trial. Not satisfied with the carnage he had already left behind in this West Texas town, in an attempted jail break on November 18, 1929, using a pistol he had taken, Ratliff fatally shot long-time area peace officer jailer "Uncle Tom" Jones. Hearing of the death of their beloved lawman, the next morning a mob appeared at the jail. While in conversation with the jailer on duty, the mob was able to overpower the officer and take his keys. The convicted "Santa Claus" was taken to a nearby vacant lot where an attempt was made to hang him on a guy wire between two utility poles. The rope broke, but a larger rope was obtained and in the second try "Santa Claus" died!

Texas Embassy in London

Anyone who has ever seriously cracked a Texas history book is aware that the Republic of Texas ratified a treaty with England in 1842. This bit of foreign diplomacy was negotiated by James Hamilton in 1840. This made Texas the only state with which England had separate and ratified treaty relations. What fewer Texans know is that it took 121 years for the Texas embassy in London to have a proper marker.

And, as an additional surprise, this was done in part by the efforts of the architect who designed Dallas' well-known Magnolia (Mobil Oil) building, where the company's logo, Pegasus, "the Flying Red Horse," has welcomed folks to Dallas since 1934. English architect Alfred Bossom, the building's designer, along with other Britains with Texas ties, was instrumental in founding the Anglo-Texan Society.

The building at 3 St. James Street that housed the offices of the charge d'affaires to the Court of St. James, Dr. Ashbel Smith, 1842-1845. (Photo courtesy of Mary G. Ramos)

In 1953 Sir Bossom, the architect of numerous sky-scrapers in America, joined in the movement to form such a society as a social club and to foster a good relationship between England and Texas. When it was learned that the Republic of Texas legation, occupied by Sam Houston's appointee as Minister to the Court of St. James, Dr. Ashbel Smith M.D., had gone since 1842 unmarked, it was decided that an undertaking should be made to do so. The legation was located in an upstairs room at No. 3 St. James street, which today is above one of England's most venerable wine and spirits producers, the makers of Cutty Sark whiskey. After a detailed research of the Republic of Texas legation in London, the Society enlisted the services of the then Texas governor Price Daniel, whose expertise was solicited in obtaining a proper marker for the old legation. This included a discussion as to the material to be used for the marker. While some preferred Texas mesquite wood and others wanted granite, it was determined the marker would be made of cast aluminum by the Southwell Company of San Antonio, the makers of Texas historical markers since 1930. Below the seal of the Republic of Texas is the following text:

TEXAS LEGATION

In this building was the legation for
the ministers from the Republic of Texas
to the Court of St. James 1842-1845
Erected by the ANGLO-TEXAS SOCIETY

The plaque was unveiled by Governor Daniel in August 1963.

Nine Flags Over Nacogdoches

While most Texans are aware that their state has been, during its existence, under six flags, one of the state's oldest and most historically rich towns, the East Texas town of Nacogdoches, has an annual festival celebrating its existence under nine flags. The town was named for the Nacadoche Indians who originally inhabited the area. The town's antiquity, according to the *Handbook of Texas*, "is indicated by the presence of four Indian mounds within the city limits." The town's first European settlement was made in June of 1716.

In addition to the well-known six flags that flew over Texas: Spain, France, Mexico, The Republic of Texas, The Confederacy, and the United States; the town was under the yoke of three lessor known flags, at least for a brief period of time.

The town, which at the beginning of the nineteenth century was the largest city in Texas, figured in several important events in the history of Texas, three of which resulted in its subjugation to three additional flags.

In 1812, in a plan to free Texas from Spanish rule, Jose Gutierrez De Lara initiated a filibustering expedition assisted by a West Point graduate, Augustus McGee, in what was known as the Gutierrez-McGee Expedition. Marching under the Expedition's green flag of the "Republic of the North," the expedition entered Nacogdoches on August 12, 1812. For a brief period the flag of the "Republic of the North" flew over Nacogdoches.

On June 17, 1819, Dr. James Long, with several followers, entered Texas and occupied Nacogdoches' Old Stone Fort. He organized a provisional government, which he called "The Republic of Texas." After the defeat of the Long Expedition, which was formed to oppose the boundary of the Louisiana Purchase, Nacogdoches was to fall victim to yet a third campaign of aggression.

On December 16, 1826, the town fell victim to what is known as the Fredonian Rebellion. Angered by a controversy between Mexican authorities and impresario Haden Edwards, Benjamin Edwards and about thirty followers rode into Nacogdoches under a flag inscribed, "Independence, Liberty, and Justice." And seizing the Old Stone Fort, they proclaimed it the Republic of Fredonia. This gave the town its ninth flag.

Dallas Entertainment Quarter, Home of City's Historical Brewery

Aside from its many faceted venues of Dallas nightlife and eateries, Dallas' modern focal point of entertainment known as "the West End" has, hidden behind its neon-lit,

Nestled snugly in the shadows of Dallas' towering skyscrapers is an antique building known to those who frequent the West End as The Brewery. This historic building once housed one of Dallas' earliest industries, The Dallas Brewery. It was here that Anton Wagenhaeuser brewed Dallas Beer, of which he said, "There is none finer." (Photo by Marianne Cannon)

aging brick facades, a story of early Dallas known only to those historians and researchers who have rummaged through the faded and yellowed pages of deeds and early documents pertaining to Dallas' adolescent years. A clue to this story can be observed from the freeways and feeder streets that funnel traffic into the heart of downtown Dallas.

If one looks in the direction of Dallas' low-lying western skyline, one can hardly miss seeing an antique-looking gray building identified by a large black sign with white block letters as "THE BREWERY." Behind and beneath this sign lies a tale worth pointing out to visitors who may think our city's early history revolves around the "Old Red Courthouse." Although not as imposing, this building identified as The Brewery is really the heart of one of Dallas' most famous business ventures.

First of all, the antiquated structure sits on land that once belonged to early Dallas settler Sarah Cockrell. This enterprising woman built the first iron bridge over the Trinity River. The property was sold in 1884 to Anton Wagenhaeuser, who built the Wagenhaeuser Brewery. In 1885 the brewery became known as the Dallas Brewery. As a direct result of Prohibition, Dallas Brewery changed its name and product line, becoming the Grain Juice Company.

By 1927 it was known as the Morgan Warehouse and Commercial Company. The Dallas Brewery that once proudly advertised, "Dallas Beer has no equal" was no more. In 1947 the old brewery became the Alford Terminal Warehouses, a forerunner to the Alford family's Alford Refrigerated Warehouse of today.

In its final stages, the infamous Dallas Schoolbook Depository, from which Lee Harvey Oswald allegedly shot

President John F. Kennedy, leased the historic old building to supplement its facility on the corner of Elm and Houston Streets.

Going Up in Smoke! (Tobacco Auctioneers on Texas Horizon?)

Industry, Texas, in Austin County on the edge of the Texas Hill Country was founded in 1838 by Friedrich Ernst and Charles Fordtran, who had immigrated to New York from Germany. Glowing accounts of Stephen F. Austin's colony in Texas drew them to Central Texas. Ernst received title to a league of land, which he divided with Fordtran, who surveyed it. Letters from the men to friends in Germany persuaded others to immigrate to the area, and in 1838 Ernst laid out a town site.

German immigrants visiting the Ernst home convinced him to make cigars from the tobacco he had grown in his Texas garden. The cigar industry, which developed from this ignoble start, gave the community its name.

While these German immigrants may have been the first colonists to grow tobacco on Texas soil, they do not have a lock on this distinct honor. A Dallas County tobacconist, who is an immigrant from Iran, Pfast Eddy Barahmi, is well on his way to turning a pipe dream into an entrepreneurial reality. This man's Addison tobacco shop, Cigar Shop and More, features hand-rolled cigars. Pfast Eddy's house brand bears a cigar ring decorated by his appropriate logo, a red cowboy boot with winged heels.

Eddy has already proved that North Texas soil is suitable for producing fine smoking tobacco. The man with a name that sounds more like a racetrack devotee' or the owner of an

Demonstrating his cigar rolling skill is Jose Antonio Perez, a Cuban master cigar roller who has hand rolled cigars for forty-seven years. He rolls cigars for Pfast Eddy, a Dallas area tobacconist who has successfully grown tobacco in North Texas. (Photo by Marianne Cannon)

auto dealership than the stodgy image we associate with places like "Ye Olde Tobacco Shoppe" has already produced tobacco in Texas soil for several years. It is his belief that just as wine racks across the country proudly offer Texas-grown wines, the new century will not be very old before the humidors of discriminating smokers will contain fine cigars made with Texas-grown tobacco. Hopefully, he inserted, encircled with the cigar band bearing the red cowboy boot with Pfast Eddy's winged heels.

Death by the Rope in Dallas

Before 1914 when the "new" Dallas County jail and Criminal Courts Building was opened, the Dallas County jail was located on Houston Street near where the Union Terminal Station is presently located. Just outside the jail were the gallows where until the 1920s, when the state assumed the responsibility for executing the state's condemned prisoners, public hangings were carried out. Across the way, where the Dallas Morning News building and Ferris Plaza stands, was a wagon yard where spectators gathered to watch the condemned swing. The show stopped when prisoners were moved to the newly constructed jail just down the street at Main and Houston Streets. Hangings were carried out there for the next decade. Although the old gallows were lost to renovation, the death cells can still be seen there.

A history of the Dallas County Sheriff's Office informs us that in 1853 Sheriff Trezevant C. Hawpe presided over Dallas County's first legal hanging. The condemned was a black woman named "Jane." She was convicted of splitting open with an ax the head of a widower named Wisdom, who had hired her to take care of the house and his children.

The Five States of Texas?

Biographers say Texas politician and former vice president of the United States John Nance (Cactus Jack) Garner of Uvalde, Texas, introduced a bill in the 1899 session of the Texas legislature which, if passed, would have divided Texas into five states. His stated reasoning was to "increase Lone Star representation in the United States Congress." Although the idea of dividing Texas sounds preposterous if not down-right treasonous to the average Texan, Garner's idea was not without foundation. According to the book *Annexation of Texas*, published in 1919, "The resolution of Congress allowing the annexation of Texas had the provision that Texas could be divided into states of a convenient size not to exceed four in addition to the said state of Texas." This verbiage allows for five states. Garner's proposal did not pass.

Texians Become Santa Anna's Savior

The resentful and vengeful brutality of Mexican general Antonio Lopez de Santa Anna toward the rebellious Texas colonists is underscored by his using his army band to sound the *deguello* on the morning of March 6, 1836, at the Alamo. This blood-curdling piece of music was his signal for his troops to attack the Spanish mission. But it had far more significance for the handful of defenders than just the start of the attack. The *Handbook of Texas* reminds us that "the deguello signifies the act of beheading or throat cutting, and in Spanish history became associated with the meaning of complete destruction of the enemy without mercy!"

From the day the general commanded the red flag meaning "give no quarter" be raised over the city of San Antonio, which was in plain sight by the Alamo defenders, the Texians knew that if they lost, their fate was sealed. This, along with his other atrocities, such as the massacre at Goliad, made the Mexican leader a monster to be reckoned with in the eyes of all Texians.

And yet, from the time he was captured following the battle of San Jacinto, much effort was made to keep the despised purveyor of inhuman suffering alive. The first example of mercy being shown to the vanquished general occurred immediately after his capture at San Jacinto. When his disguise was unsuccessful and he was identified, he was brought before General Sam Houston. Many of Houston's men demanded that he be executed immediately. But this was not to be. The Mexican general, knowing that both himself and Sam Houston were members of the Masonic lodge exploited this fraternal relationship and asked Houston to spare his life. Houston intervened and the commander of the Mexican forces was spared.

This was not to be Santa Anna's last brush with death at the hands of the Texians. David G. Burnet, who served as interim president of the fledgling republic was faced with numerous problems facing the Republic of Texas. Historians have said that perhaps Burnet's most important service during the eight months he was president was keeping Santa Anna alive! Had many military men had their way, he would have been killed. If this had happened, the newly won republic would have incurred the disfavor of many nations whose friendship was needed by the fragile new nation.

The Day the Flag Came Down

Anson Jones was the last president of the Republic of Texas. He served from December 9, 1844, to February 19, 1846, when he carved a special niche for himself in Texas history by lowering the Lone Star flag of the Republic. Jones is credited with achieving annexation of Texas by the United States. In announcing the death of the Republic on February 16, 1846, at the capitol in Austin, Jones is quoted as saying,

> The Lone Star of Texas, which ten years ago rose amid clouds over fields of carnage, obscurely seen for a while, has culminated, and following an inscrutable destiny, has passed on and become fixed forever in that constellation which all free men and lovers of freedom in the world must reverence and adore, the American union. . . . The final act in the great drama is performed. The Republic of Texas is no more!

It has been written that as Jones lowered the flag of the Republic, its pole broke.

Texas' Big Real Estate Deal of 1850

The treaty settling land disputes between Mexico and Texas and ending the Mexican-American War in 1848 resulted in Texas acquiring vast land holdings which included much of present New Mexico, Colorado, and portions of Oklahoma, Kansas, and a smidgen of Wyoming. Texas divested itself of all lands outside its present boundaries when the Compromise of 1850 allowed the United States to acquire this land for ten million dollars in an interest-bearing note. The act ceding this land to the

United States was ratified by the Texas Legislature and signed by Governor Peter H. Bell on November 25, 1850. Before this land was ceded to the U.S., Colorado's now popular ski resort Crested Butte was in Texas.

Fabled Judge Roy Bean Renders TKO to Prizefight Law

Charles Allen Culberson, the twenty-first governor of the state of Texas, served from January 15, 1895, to January 17, 1899. In 1895 Culberson convened the legislature to prohibit prizefighting in Texas after plans had been made for the Jim Corbett-Bob Fitzsimmons match to be held in Dallas before a crowd of 53,000. He called the match "an act of public barbarism." A court had held that prizefighting did not violate the law; the legislative bill was passed prohibiting prizefighting in Texas.

But the governor was to learn that the sparring had just begun. The Fitzsimmons-Corbett match was moved to Carson City Nevada where Corbett was defeated. Culberson later asked the Rangers to keep the Fitzsimmons-Maher fight from being held in Texas.

Judge Roy Bean, known as "the Law West of the Pecos," used his personal style of fancy footwork to circumvent the law the following year when he staged the Fitzsimmons-Maher heavyweight championship fight in a ring built on a sandbar in the bed of the Rio Grande just below Langtry on February 21, 1896. The bout had been forbidden in Texas, New Mexico, and Arizona. By building his ring across the river in Mexican territory, Bean outwitted the Rangers who had been dispatched to stop him.

Famous Helper

Clara Barton, founder of the American Red Cross, personally directed relief work at the Galveston flood of 1900.

Humble Beginnings

The Mobley Hotel in Cisco, Texas, was bought in 1919 by Conrad Hilton and became the first hotel in the Hilton chain.

The Spanish Vara

The vara is a Spanish unit of distance used in Spanish and Mexican surveys and land grants in Texas. One vara equals approximately 33 1/3 inches; 5,645.4 square varas equal an acre; 1,906.1 varas equal a mile.

Originally in Spanish the word meant "the long, thin, clean branch of a tree or plant." Later it came to be used as any straight stick or lance. It was also a badge of office when carried by a mayor or judge. It began being used as a measuring stick and eventually as a measurement.

Sunday Houses

The building of Sunday houses is believed to have originated in the Hill Country town of Fredericksburg. Upon their arrival, German settlers were given a half-acre town lot and a ten-acre farm plot. As there were no rural stores or churches, it was sometimes necessary for families to stay in town for several days at a time to trade and to attend church. This was especially true on special days such as

Easter and Christmas. Some colonists used their town lots to build houses for staying over in town. These were called "Sunday Houses."

First Female Telegrapher in America?

Nine-year-old Hallie Hutchinson, who lived in the Williams Ranch community of Mills County, Texas, may very well have been America's first female telegraph operator. She was the daughter of Captain A. A. Hutchinson, who in 1874 built the first hotel in Mills County. Captain Hutchinson came from Florida and named the hotel the Florida Hotel, but it was best known as the "Hutch Hotel."

When the first telegraph line in that part of the country was established, the telegraph office was installed in the hotel. Little Hallie was the office's first part-time telegraph operator. The telegraph ran between Austin and Fort Concho. The line was strung along Military Road, which, as a result, was later known as Wire Road.

First Auto Trip in Texas Affords a Trove of Trivia

The first gasoline-engine automobile in Texas belonged to one-legged Col. E.H.R. "Ned" Green. The automobile was a Phaeton runabout built by the St. Louis Gas Car Co. It had a two-cylinder engine, tiller, and buggy top. The cost to Col. Green for this 1899 model St. Louis was $1,260. This was more than a year's salary for most Texans. Col. Green could well afford the new addition to Texas roads, such as they were in those days, as Col. Green was the son of Hetty Green, the so-called "Witch of Wall Street," who was said to be the richest woman in the world. The "horseless carriage" was shipped to Green by its designer, George P. Dorris, who accompanied Green on the first automobile trip in Texas. The trip from Terrell, Texas, Green's home, to Dallas, where Green maintained an apartment, a distance of thirty miles, took the pair five hours in October of 1899. About one hour of that was taken up in the small town of Forney, where the **first automobile accident** in Texas occurred.

According to an article in the *Dallas Morning News*, "a farm wagon crowded Green's automobile off the road and into a gully damaging it." This was, no doubt, Texas' first automobile accident. The *News* article also informs us that the accident produced Texas' **first automobile repairman** as well. "A stop at a blacksmith's shop operated by Henry Reeve, an African-American who operated shops in Forney from the turn of the century until 1920, resulted in Henry being Texas' first auto repairman."

After the accident and subsequent repairs, Green and Dorris left Forney in their St. Louis and proceeded at less than breakneck speeds to Dallas. Green was quoted as saying, "We did not put on full power on country roads. When we struck the asphalt pavement on Main Street [in Dallas], we dared not do so because the thoroughfare was so crowded it would have been dangerous to human life."

The vehicle, built like a Phaeton (buggy), was propelled by a five-horsepower engine that consumed two quarts of gasoline on the trip from Terrell to Dallas. Its tank held three gallons. The importance of this initial run of a gasoline-powered "horseless carriage" was that it introduced to our state a new era of transportation that during the next ninety years would change the lives of the people of the state.

Hammering Out the Declaration of Independence

Historians write that Noah Turner Byers, who immigrated to Texas from South Carolina in 1835, opened a blacksmith shop in Washington-on-the-Brazos. The convention of 1836, which wrote the declaration of independence for Texas and instituted an ad interim government of the Republic of Texas, is said to have held its sessions at Byers' shop. One can say that the important declaration was "hammered out" at the blacksmith shop.

New London School Disaster

What has been called the "greatest school disaster in the United States" occurred on the afternoon of March 18, 1937, when 293 students, teachers, and visitors were killed when a natural gas explosion destroyed the New London, Texas school. A natural gas leak caused natural gas to accumulate under the building. The leak went undetected because, at the time, natural gas was colorless and odorless.

It was this horrendous incident that resulted in today's natural gas having its pungent smell. The disaster prompted legislation requiring natural gas to have an additive to give it an unpleasant odor, making it easily detected. Mr. Carl Huff of Texas Utilities, which owns Lone Star Gas Company, advises that since then his company has used mercaptan to give the fuel its unpleasant odor.

One of the first reporters on the scene in the East Texas town was a temporary relief reporter in the Dallas bureau of the United Press news service. His name was Walter Cronkite. The disaster touched the life of this reporter, who would one day become a household word as a television news celebrity. In his biography, Mr. Cronkite wrote how, upon arrival at the school, the destruction and carnage was apparent, as was the frantic search for loved ones.

Gunslinging Doc

Dr. John H. "Doc" Holliday, the notorious gambler and gunslinger who was a friend of Wyatt Earp of Tombstone, Arizona, fame, once practiced dentistry in the city of Dallas.

"El Castile" a Victorian Showpiece in Cattle Country

Sitting on a slight rise overlooking Decatur, county seat of Wise County, one of the first things that meets the eye, vying for attention with the magnificent historic Wise County courthouse, is the majestic Victorian home of Texas cattle baron Dan Waggoner. Somewhat eerie in its emptiness, at first sight, this ornately decorated structure virtually commands one to take notice. This stone mansion from another time is known locally as simply "the Waggoner Mansion."

Built by cattle baron Dan Waggoner in 1883, everyone in Decatur assumes everyone knows who Dan Waggoner was! A review of our *Handbook of Texas* reminds us that Daniel Waggoner was born in Lincoln County, Tennessee, in 1828. His family moved to Hopkins County, Texas, in the 1840s. In about 1850 Dan Waggoner took a small herd of longhorns and located on Denton Creek in Wise County. In 1851 he bought 15,000 acres on the Trinity 18 miles west of present Decatur. Indian marauders were so bad in that region he returned to Denton Creek. After the death of his first wife, he married Ann Halsell of Wise County in 1859.

Waggoner was a successful rancher, and in 1870 he and his son drove a herd of cattle to market in Kansas. He returned with the proceeds of the sale and began the expanding of the Waggoner Ranch, which eventually extended into several counties. The Waggoner (Three D) Ranch, which began on Cactus Hill in Wise County, started breeding shorthorns and Herefords, as well as fine horses. The Waggoners were responsible for building the famous Arlington Downs racetrack and stables between Fort Worth and Dallas, where fine horses were bred.

Built in 1883, the Waggoner Mansion, with its commanding view of Decatur, is truly a Victorian showpiece in Texas cattle country. (Photo by Marianne Cannon)

The Waggoner Mansion has been lived in as late as 1950. It is now owned by Decatur residents, the Lukers. While the wrought iron entrance gate bears the name El Castile, which in Spanish means The Castle, and while the intriguing old structure is certainly qualified for such a noble name, Rosalie Gregg of the Wise County Historical Society told us he might have called his home that, but she is not sure he did.

The new *Handbook of Texas* reviews El Castile as follows: "On a rocky hill overlooking Decatur, Daniel Waggoner carefully trained his son to handle stock and supervise the ranch." This information seems to verify that the entire home site, which fits the book's description, was known as El Castile. Even though Dan Waggoner made his first real money in the cattle business while living in Wise County, the Waggoner Ranch moved further west after he built his home in Decatur. Waggoner died in 1904.

Dallas and the Central National Road of the Republic of Texas

The Central National Road was planned by the Texas Congress, which, on February 5, 1844, selected a five-man commission to select a right of way, see that it was cleared, and supervise the building of necessary bridges. The road was to begin at the bank of the Trinity River not more than fifteen miles below the Elm fork, Dallas County, and run to the northwest corner of Red River County. As surveyed, the Central Road probably started at the John Neely Bryan crossing on the Trinity River, a little north of the later site of the Dallas County courthouse, ran east by north to the Dallas County line, and continued north until it reached the extreme northwest corner of Red River County. With its connections to other existing roads, including the road between Austin and Preston Bend on the Red River, the Central National Road became truly an international highway between St. Louis and San Antonio.

The history of the Central National Road can be found in the shadows of its starting point, the John Neely Bryan cabin. A historical marker telling of this important transportation route can be found in the heart of Dallas' entertainment center known as The West End. The historical old road probably ran through the center of this enclave of nightclubs and chic restaurants.

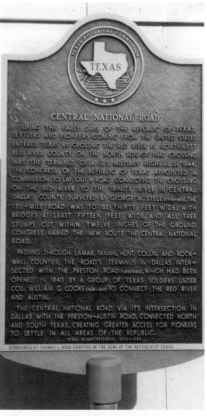

One of Texas' first, if not the first, Interstate highways is marked by this historical marker tucked away in Dallas' West End entertainment quarter. (Photo by Marianne Cannon)

Texas City Remembered

April 16, 1947, was the day the Texas Gulf Coast shook and all of Texas shuddered from the resulting shock waves! For those of us having any personal connection to the Texas City Disaster, it will, as President Roosevelt said of Pearl Harbor, "be a day that lives in infamy."

I was a senior in high school and working part-time at a Dallas funeral home. I recall how management came around to all the employees on duty, especially the embalmers, and alerted us that some of the employees might be called upon to go to Texas City to assist in various ways and to tend to the vast number of casualties that were the result of what the *Handbook of Texas* called, "One of the worst disasters in Texas' history."

The SS Grandecamp wallows in debris alongside its Texas City dock following its disastrous explosion.

Pretty impressive on a young adult of my age. Details of that day may have dimmed with time in comparison to the impact the news reports on the radio made that day, so I am glad I can call upon the *Handbook of Texas* for a description of these events. "At 9:12 A.M. the ship SS *Grandecamp*, a French-owned vessel loaded with the highly explosive fertilizer ammonium nitrate, which caught fire early in the morning, exploded while attempts were being made to extinguish the fire. The entire dock area was destroyed, along with the nearby Monsanto Chemical Company and other smaller companies and warehouses. Also destroyed were numerous oil and chemical tanks. Smaller explosions and fires were ignited by flying debris, not only along the industrial area but also throughout the city. A fifteen-foot tidal wave created by the force swept the dock area. The concussion of the explosion, felt as far away as Port Arthur, damaged or destroyed at least 1,000 residences and buildings throughout Texas City.

"The ship SS *High Flyer*, in dock for repairs and also carrying ammonium nitrate, had been ignited by the first explosion. It was towed 100 feet from the docks before it exploded, sixteen hours later at 1:10 A.M. on April 17. The first explosion had killed 26 Texas City firemen and destroyed all the city's fire fighting equipment, including four fire trucks, leaving the city helpless in the wake of the second explosion. Probably the exact number of people killed will never be known. Hundreds of local volunteers began fighting fires and doing rescue work."

Red Cross personnel and volunteers from surrounding cities responded with assistance, until almost 4,000 workers were operating. Temporary hospitals, morgues, and shelters were set up.

The ship's anchor monument records 576 persons dead, 398 of whom were identified and 178 were listed as missing. The injured ranged in the thousands. I later saw records that said that over 3,500 were injured. All records of personnel and payroll at Monsanto Chemical Company were destroyed, and many of the dock workers were itinerants, making identification almost impossible in that area. Firemen, ship's crew, and spectators were killed! And most of the bodies were never recovered. Sixty-three bodies were buried unidentified. The loss of property, according to the *Handbook of Texas*, totaled $67 million.

Litigation over the Texas City disaster was finally settled in 1962 when the United States Supreme Court refused to review an appeal court's ruling that the Republic of France, owner of the SS *Grandecamp,* could not be held liable for claims resulting from the explosion.

The Sabine as a Border

When Texans think of an international border, as related to Texas, they automatically think of the Rio Grande as border between Mexico and Texas. One other Texas river has seen service as an international border. The Sabine, which means cypress in Spanish, makes up two-thirds of the border between Louisiana and Texas and has served in this capacity. The 360-mile-long river served as international border between U.S. and Spain, U.S. and Mexico, and U.S. and the Republic of Texas.

Courthouse Moved by Cowboys

A 1903 election moved the county seat of Hartley County from Hartley to Channing, which was the headquarters of the famed XIT Ranch. The Panhandle county was the scene of an ahead-of-its-time transportation feat! Enterprising cowboys from the XIT put the old frame courthouse on wheels and towed it behind their horses to the new county seat. The old courthouse was transformed into a hotel when a new brick courthouse was constructed in 1906.

Sam Houston's Paid Forger

The Dallas Historical Society writes that the first currency authorized by the Republic of Texas circulated in the fall of 1837. People called this "star money" because of the star printed on the bill. This money was easy to counterfeit, however, and it was replaced in January of 1838.

"Each new bill in the 1837 and the 1838 series was signed by the Secretary of the Treasury and the President. President Sam Houston did not sign the 1837 series, himself, though, because of a physical disability. He had an injured hand. Instead, his name was signed by William G. Cooke, who was paid 2 cents for each signature."

Texas and the American Revolution

Bernardo de Galvez, for whom Galveston Island is named, was, according to the *Handbook of Texas*, governor of Louisiana from 1777 until 1783. He is recognized for his aid to the Americans during the American Revolution. He recognized the independence of the United States and captured Florida from the British. He also asked the Spanish governor of Texas to support the Americans by sending beef from the Spanish army. Cattle were sent from several Texas missions. This made Texas one of the few states west of the Mississippi to participate in the cause of the Americans in the Revolution.

Deathbed Loyalty

Although one Sam Houston biography claims the general's last deathbed words were "Texas, Texas, Margaret" The most accepted last words attributed to the Texas hero was "Texas!"

"Grave of the Confederacy"

In May of 1865, just after the collapse of the Confederacy, Gen. Joseph Orville Shelby, commander of the Missouri Raiders, who was stationed in Texas at the time of Robert E. Lee's surrender, led his brigade across Texas and into Mexico in what was known as the Shelby Expedition. Shelby had refused to surrender.

His troop strength was variously estimated at from three thousand to twelve thousand men. When some one thousand of them reached Piedras Negras, they buried their Confederate flag in the Rio Grande in a ceremony which came to be described as "the grave of the Confederacy incident."

Neutral Ground in Texas

Unable to agree on the boundary between Louisiana and Texas following the Louisiana Purchase, the United States and Spain, in order to avert an armed clash, met on November 6, 1806, and declared the disputed territory Neutral Ground. Although never officially set, the boundaries were considered to be the Arroyo Hondo on the east and the Sabine River on the west. One must assume that the southern boundary was the Gulf of Mexico. The 32nd parallel latitude formed the northern boundary.

Although America and Spain both stipulated in the agreement that no settlers would be permitted in the Neutral Ground, settlers from both Spanish and American territories moved in. In addition, outlaws found the area good for their nefarious activities. In 1810 both countries found it necessary to send in joint military expeditions to expel the outlaws, who were making travel and trade dangerous. Ownership of the strip of land went to the United States by the Adams-Onis Treaty of 1821.

"Pecosin'" a Feared Word

Back when law was practically nonexistent in the two-fisted, gun-totin' days of the region around the Pecos River, the term "Pecosin'" meant to dispose of a killing victim by throwing his body in the Pecos. The term had a definite ring of finality to it!

"Jackass Mail"

Because road conditions during the days of the Republic of Texas were so poor, with almost no bridges, even stage travel was undesirable. The discovery of gold on the west coast in 1849 brought about several reasonably reliable stage lines to carry passengers, freight, and mail. One line between San Antonio and El Paso used primarily mules for power and was quickly dubbed "The Jackass Mail."

San Angelo or Santa Angela?

A case of federal nitpicking resulted in a city's name change. Bart Dewitte's trading post, around which the city was formed, was originally called Santa Angela in honor of Mr. Dewitte's sister, a Mexican nun. The name was Anglicized to St. Angela, and finally to San Angelo when the federal government, issuing a bank charter and establishing a post office, objected to the masculine San and the feminine Angela.

"Spruce Goose"

The "Spruce Goose" was a gigantic, eight-engine flying boat built in the 1940s by Houston-born eccentric billionaire Howard Hughes, son of Howard R. Hughes, founder of Hughes Tool Company. Hughes, who started flying at age fourteen set several world records, including flying around the world in 91 hours and 14 minutes.

The "Spruce Goose" was constructed of plywood. It had an enormous wingspan of 319 feet. It was designed to hold 700 passengers. The one and only time the plane was flown was in 1947 when Hughes, to verify the unusual craft would hold together, taxied the plane out on the water. When the plane did hold together, Hughes gave the plane enough power to lift it into the air. The airplane was airborne for one mile at an altitude of 70 feet. This brief test was the craft's only flight. It was then moved to San Francisco Bay in California, where it was put on display for public exhibition. Hughes, who achieved notoriety for his eccentric behavior, died a recluse in 1976.

Twentieth-Century Cattle Brand

Although we tend to think of cattle branding as a symbol of early Texas ranches and trail herds, this practice was continued into the twentieth century. One of the little known examples of modern day cattle branding involves a well-known Dallas institution, the Buckner Orphan's Home. In her biography of "Father" R.C. Buckner, entitled, *Homeward Bound*, Karen Bullock writes, in discussing the year 1947, "This was the year Buckner's own brand, BOH, was used to identify ninety-three head of cattle that Lacy Sanctuary purchased the year before."

Fort Worth's Casa Manana, a Product of Neighborly Rivalry

In 1924 a permanent Texas Centennial committee was approved to make plans to celebrate the 100th anniversary of Texas independence. Dallas was chosen as the site for the Centennial celebration. The selection of Dallas inflamed the already existing friendly rivalry between that city and its westerly neighbor, Fort Worth. It especially ruffled the feathers of businessman and Fort Worth booster Amon Carter. That rivalry spawned a project that is alive and well today in the "city where the West begins." The rivalry helped bring about Casa Manana (House of Tomorrow). The year-round, air-conditioned, aluminum-domed, theater-in-the-round was not the original Casa Manana.

Already rankled by the selection of Dallas as the site for the Centennial celebration, Amon Carter signed the famous Broadway producer Billy Rose at $1,000 a day for 100 days to produce the "show of shows" for Fort Worth. History of the Casa tells us how in a few days a pasture was transformed into 40 magic acres housing the largest revolving stage and café in the world. It accommodated 4,000 diners and dancers. It ran for four consecutive years.

Today, only memories remain of its grandeur. In 1945 a bond election included $500,000 for building a recreation center and amphitheater, however, financial considerations caused the matter to be delayed for twelve years. The project was brought to life again in 1957 by the late James Snowden, Fort Worth oilman. He was instrumental in moving the city council to build today's theater-in-the-round. Construction began in March of 1958; 114 days later the theater opened its first season.

The Georgia Army

The so-called Georgia army was a citizens' group organized in the almost lawless Montague County in about 1872 to suppress unlawful activities in the county. The group, composed mainly of southern-born citizens, was under the leadership of a man named Williamson from the state of Georgia. Members of the Georgia army road the county for about a week strongly suggesting to undesirable residents that they leave the area. The sheriff resigned at the suggestion of the Georgia army. Historical accounts of these events tell us that following these actions, conditions in Montague County improved.

"Honor Thy Father and Mother"

This biblical admonition seems to have been taken quite literally by the founding fathers of Navarro County! Corsicana, their county seat, was named for the Mediterranean Sea island of Corsica, which was the home of the parents of José Antonio Navarro, for which the county was named.

Executions in Texas

The execution by hanging of Roy Mitchell in Waco on July 30, 1923, marked an end to hanging as the form of legal executions in Texas. Prior to the 1920s, each county was responsible for executing those sentenced to die in their county, where hanging was the accepted form of execution. In the 1920s the state legislature passed laws which moved all executions to the Texas Department of Corrections in Huntsville. The electric chair was selected as the preferred form of execution.

Chicago Was Once in Texas

Originally, according to the *Handbook of Texas*, Lamesa in Dawson County was named Chicago when it was established as the county seat in 1905. When the post office was established in March of 1905, the name was changed to

Lamesa from the Spanish description of the flat tableland on which it was situated.

Famous Last Words

Although "famous last words" are usually in reference to the last utterances of someone on their death bed, one of the most notable "famous last words" recorded are very much a part of our Texas heritage worth remembering! Anson Jones, the last president of the Republic of Texas, on February 19, 1846, ushering in the new state of Texas as part of the union, declared, "The Republic of Texas is no more!" He then retired to Barrington, his plantation near Washington-on-the-Brazos.

"Treue Der Union" Comfort, Texas

It is doubtful that one can find a more deserved monument to patriotism in Texas than the one that stands in the Hill Country town of Comfort. This Kendall County town was settled by Germans from the town of New Braunfels in 1854. Wearied by their journey, they were charmed by the scenery and sparkling water. They called the place "Camp Comfort."

The outbreak of the Civil War divided Texans into two camps, Secessionists and Union sympathizers (those, like Sam Houston, who wanted to avoid splitting the Union). A band of residents of Comfort, mostly Germans, who were Unionists left Comfort en route to Mexico. On August 10, 1862, the sixty-five men encamped on the Nueces River were attacked by ninety-four mounted Confederate soldiers. Nineteen Unionists were killed and nine were wounded. The wounded were executed later. Of the thirty-seven who escaped the battle, six were killed while trying to cross into Mexico. Eleven reached home, and most of the remaining twenty escaped temporarily to Mexico or California. The monument "Treue der Union" (True to the Union) commemorates the battle of the Nueces and bears the names of the victims of the battle.

Fort Tenoxtitlan, a Mexican Exercise in Futility

Located in present Burleson County, Fort Tenoxtitlan was one in a chain of military garrisons built by the Mexicans to enforce the law of April 6, 1830, restricting immigration from the United States into Texas. The fort's commander reported to Mexico City that the restrictions were unenforceable. The anti-immigration laws were repealed in May of 1834.

On the Road Again, Texas Highway Trivia

Space does not allow us to print all of the unusual facts surrounding the miles and miles of highways and roads that spider-web our enormous state. We can, however, review a few facts about the ribbons of pavement kept in shape by our Texas Department of Transportation (formerly Texas Highway Department). A good beginning is to tell the long and the short of highway facts.

The longest highway in Texas is Interstate 10 running east to west. The highway is 878.7 miles long. Texas' shortest highway is located in Teneha, Texas, in Shelby County. It is a highway loop that measures .074 miles or 391 feet long. Texas' first paved highway was a brick road built while

Governor James (Farmer Jim) Ferguson was in office. It extended some sixty miles from the governor's home in Temple to his ranch in Bosque County.

Montague County is the venue of a great highway story that should be included in all "Texas Brag" conversations. "Thars gold in them thar roads" could truthfully be the cry of Montague County residents. Though folks living in or near the town of Ringold sport neither halos nor wings (as far as we know), they do reside where roads are paved with gold. In 1936, when U.S. 81 and a portion of U.S. 287 were being paved, workers from the Texas Highway Department discovered the glittering sand they used to make concrete contained gold dust. A Fort Worth laboratory assayed the value of the ore, which came from a nearby pit, at .54 per ton—far less than the cost of extracting the precious metal from the sand. A historical marker on U.S. 81 near Ringold says, "39 miles of roadway holds an estimated $31,000 in gold."

Historic Painting Very Revealing

William H. Huddle's 1886 painting "Surrender of Santa Anna" depicts a scene following the Battle of San Jacinto that reveals much to the eyes of Texas historians. The painting shows General Sam Houston sitting under a tree and surrounded by a group of his comrades-in-arms. One figure dressed in buckskin seems to be intent on hearing what his commander is saying. One hand is cupped around one ear. It is believed by some that this man was trusted Indian scout Erastus "Deaf" Smith.

One can easily see that Houston's right leg is wrapped snugly in a bandage. Our review of the history of the Battle of San Jacinto tells us that the general's leg was shattered by a bullet just above the ankle. Houston was transported by the schooner *Flora* to New Orleans for treatment. He is reported to have written that twenty or more bone fragments were removed from the injured leg.

Rickshaws Under Texas Skies

The Texas Centennial in Dallas had one feature that, considering its uncountable sights and sounds that one had to take in, may very well have been forgotten. College boys, as a means of earning tuition as well as keeping in shape, pulled foot-weary fairgoers from street to street and plaza to plaza in rickshaws during the 1936 celebration of our state's one hundredth birthday.

Included in the eclectic music offered by the Texas Centennial was a cowboy singing group, the Sons of the Pioneers. Leonard Slye, a member of that group later changed his name to Roy Rogers and married a Uvalde, Texas songbird by the name of Dale Evans, who got her radio start singing on a Dallas morning variety show, "The Earlybirds." The show was broadcast on radio station WFAA with studios atop the Santa Fe Building on Jackson Street. The "Happy Trails" traveled by this couple is now history in the annals of Western music.

The Collision of Two Giants (The Different Visions of Sam Houston and Mirabeau B. Lamar)

Sam Houston, after traveling 500 miles across Texas, is quoted as declaring Texas the finest country to its extent upon the globe! This is not the voice of the freedom-fighter for which Houston is famous, but that of a visionary who saw Texas as a frontier offering much to settlers wanting to build a new life for themselves and for their progeny.

Mirabeau B. Lamar, second president of the Republic of Texas, who also distinguished himself on the field of battle, was a visionary of more poetic and grandiose fashion. History depicts him as a little more theatrical in his pronouncements. Lamar was a man not lacking in self-confidence, as reflected by one of his war experiences at the battle of San Jacinto. Lamar successfully rode cavalier-like into the jaws of death to rescue two comrades-in-arms. This feat did not go unnoticed. As he rode out of the Mexican lines back to his own troops, the enemy acknowledged their admiration by a volley as he passed. Reining in his horse, Lamar bowed in reply.

Escapades such as these did much to feed his self-esteem. The man for whom the Mexican army offered a salute was inaugurated as the second president of the Republic on December 10 in the old capitol, which occupied the site of the present Rice Hotel, along with his vice president, David G. Burnet. An example of him as a somewhat exaggerated visionary was his dream that Texas, with successful conquests, could be an empire with its boundary extended to the Pacific Ocean.

Historians have portrayed Vice President Burnet as sharing Lamar's trait as an exaggerated visionary or dreamer. Burnet is quoted as saying, "Texas proper is bounded by the Rio Grande; but Texas as defined by the sword may comprehend the Sierra Madre. Let the sword do its proper work!"

It was no secret that Lamar and Sam Houston were opposites. There was such bad blood between them they barely escaped dueling. One of Lamar's and Houston's greatest differences arose over Lamar's aggressive Indian policy, which included expulsion of the Cherokees from East Texas. Lamar's vindictive attitude toward the Indians flew in the face of Houston's personal relationship with the Cherokees, with whom he had lived and from whom he had received his Indian name, "The Raven." Lamar's expulsion of the Indians provoked new Indian depredations.

An indication of Houston's relationship with the Cherokees is the fact that Cherokee chief Bowles was wearing a sword and sash presented to him by Houston when he was shot and killed in the battle of the Neches in July of 1839. Cherokee warriors were mobilized by Chief Bowles as a result of Lamar ordering the normally peace-loving, nonviolent tribe's expulsion from lands along the Angelina River. This was the last battle between Cherokees and whites in Texas.

Mirabeau B. Lamar was responsible for the military supply road from La Salle County to Preston Bend on the Red River. That road connected several military forts. That road today is Dallas' prestigious and beautiful business and residential artery Preston Road. It survives while the trading town of Preston Bend lies submerged under Lake Texoma. A reminder of the old trading post town is Preston Bend, a residential subdivision on the shores of Lake Texoma near the town of Pottsboro. Nearby are the graves of Holland Coffee, whose Indian trading post was the beginning of what became Preston Bend, and his widow, Sophia Porter.

Lamar eventually turned the reins of government over to his like-minded vice president, David G. Burnet. This prompted one detractor to write, in comparing Sam Houston to Lamar and Burnet, "Drunk and in a ditch, Houston is worth a thousand Lamars and Burnets."

The "Runaway Scrape" (Texians in Flight)

The term "runaway scrape" is the term Texians applied to the flight from their homes when Mexican general Santa Anna began his effort to conquer Texas in February of 1836. The first persons involved in the flight were those residing in the south central portion of Texas, such as San Patricio, Refugio, and San Antonio. The Texians started to leave when news came that the Mexicans were gathering on the Rio Grande.

After Sam Houston learned of the fate of the Alamo, he decided to retreat and ordered all inhabitants to accompany him. People began to flee, leaving everything to make a flight to safety. Houston's retreat to regroup and find a suitable place to fight Santa Anna marked the beginning of the "Runaway Scrape."

With Houston's army gone, the settlers were left without protection from the Mexicans; the remaining settlers fled, making their way toward Louisiana or Galveston Island. Although David G. Burnet ordered Houston to halt and make a stand, Houston continued to retreat. The settler's flight was marked by a lack of preparation and panic caused by fear of both the Mexican army and the Indians. The fleeing settlers used any means of transportation or none at all. Many people died and were buried where they fell. In the meantime, Sam Houston had taken up a position with the Texian army at San Jacinto. It was there that the general made his stand against the self-proclaimed "Napoleon of the West."

The settlers' flight continued until they learned of Houston's decisive victory at San Jacinto. Because so many false rumors persisted as to the military status of the Texian army, Houston's victory was received with skepticism. But, gradually the settlers began to retrace their steps and return home. Many found their homes existed no more. The gallant thirteen-day stand of the Alamo defenders had given Houston the necessary time to regroup, decide on a place to challenge the Mexicans, and develop a strategy that resulted in his victory and independence for Texas.

Fifty Mexicans Lose Lives in "Grass Fight"

Two Texians and about fifty Mexican troops lost their lives in what became known as the "Grass Fight." Receiving minimal mention in the annals of Texas history is a bloody skirmish that proved costly to the Mexican troops occupying San Antonio. A rumor reached the Texian army that General Cos had sent Domingo de Ugartechea to Matamoros for reinforcements and silver to be used as pay for his soldiers. Scouts were sent to watch for Ugartechea's return. Erastus "Deaf" Smith spotted a pack train and troops about five miles out of San Antonio. He reported what he assumed was the returning troops and the pack train bearing what was thought to be the silver Cos had requested. On November 26, 1835, Bowie rallied about a hundred men among whom was Thomas Jefferson Rusk, later to become one of Texas' first senators.

The Texians intercepted the pack train and captured a part of the train, which bore what was assumed to be the silver. In the ensuing fight, two Texians and about fifty Mexicans lost their lives. Instead of reinforcements, however, the soldiers turned out to be a foraging party sent out to find and gather grass for the Mexican army's horses. The "bags of silver" turned out to be bags of grass to be used as fodder for the horses. The bloody battle was a costly one and all for naught!

Life Hasn't Always Been Peaches and Cream in Brenham

The Washington County seat of Brenham, known best as the home of the Blue Bell Creamery that produces the popular Blue Bell ice cream, hasn't always enjoyed the peaceful, pastoral image projected by the creamery today. Established in 1844 and incorporated in 1858, the peaceful town found itself embroiled in discord when, during the Reconstruction period following the Civil War, the town was made a military post. Federal soldiers and citizens became involved in a controversy that resulted in a partial burning of the town in 1867. Military rule lasted until 1869.

Many Germans settled in Brenham during the Reconstruction period. The Blue Bell Creamery, named for the flowers that blanketed the area, was opened in 1907. The creamery produces twenty million gallons of ice cream each year.

Dallas Revisited Through Picture Postcards

Research tells us that the height of picture postcards in the United States was in the first two decades of the twentieth century. This era was one of general prosperity and optimism in America. And picture postcards, which had been printed in the U.S. since the 1870s, gave cities and regions a way to advertise their advantages as a place to visit and to live. Although picture postcards were originally not intended to be mailed, though some were, this situation changed in 1898 when Congress reduced the postage rate for cards from two cents to one cent. This made picture postcards an ideal vehicle for Chambers of Commerce to promote their cities.

Overlooking Dallas-Oak Cliff viaduct, toward city. The longest concrete structure of its kind in the world. Cost about $700,000. Length 5,840 feet. 71 feet above low water mark.

Dallas, Texas, was not to be left out in the clamor to draw both tourists and hopefully new residents and businesses. One vintage set of folding picture postcards, touting our fair city as it appeared circa 1916 or 1917, included such astounding statistics as, "Dallas has 151.87 miles of paved streets and 279.82 miles of paved sidewalks." There were, the postcard informs the viewer, "410 business establishments in Dallas." Property value assessment was "$120,479,250." Of the thirteen color photos of Dallas street scenes, perhaps the one most revealing of this metropolis on the Trinity is a view overlooking the Dallas-Oak Cliff viaduct toward the city. The description affords the viewer with the facts that "at 5,840 feet it is the longest concrete structure of its kind in the world. Cost $700,000. It is 71 feet above the low water mark."

It was these types of scenic photos that first attracted tourists and new residents to come to Dallas to see the wonders of man's creation. For the moderate price of the postcard and its one cent mailing cost, the Chambers of Commerce in numerous cities and regions of Texas, from the Rio Grande to the Panhandle, and from the Gulf Coast to the far reaches of West Texas, reached out to America. And loved ones and friends were able to vicariously vacation and dream about one day seeing Texas in person.

Conform or Stay Home!

Early Texas settlers had many adjustments to make if they seriously considered taking advantage of land opportunities in the new frontier of Texas. Not only did they face the formidable prospects of bringing the hostile land into submission, they had to be ready to defend themselves against equally hostile Indians who were as eager to prevent the loss of their hunting lands as the settlers were of gaining land for farming and ranching.

But perhaps the most disturbing changes for many of them were imposed upon them by the Mexican government. In order to settle in Texas the settlers had to become Mexican citizens and had to be Catholic. We know that Alamo hero Jim Bowie became a Mexican citizen in 1830. He was not only a Mexican citizen but was married to a Mexican when he fought against the Mexicans at the Alamo!

Texas Wends Cling to Heritage

Although it no longer has a post office, the Lee County Wendish community of Serbin still clings to life. Its founding fathers' old rock Lutheran church still stands today, and a museum displaying evidence of the Wendish culture is one to be proud of. Texas Wends still gather annually for a Wendish reunion we were told. Wendish-German language is still spoken by some of the old-timers, both in Serbin and by others who live in the Lee County seat of Giddings, also founded by Wends. But, who are these people known as Wends? They were a Slavic people referred to as a tribe by Germans. They migrated into Germany in medieval times. Some called themselves "Sorbs."

These German-speaking outsiders were persecuted by Prussian kings for hundreds of years. Their treatment became so unbearable that in 1854, in desperation, an entire Lutheran congregation numbering 500 migrated to Texas, settling in what is today Lee County. The Wends established the community of Serbin, known as the "mother colony." Today's county seat, Giddings, was also settled by Wends. The Wends established the only Wendish newspaper in the United States, *The Deutsches Volksblatt*.

As is often the case with many rural communities, many young Wends have long since sought lifestyles in larger cities, but Lee County's Wendish progeny have elected to cling to its heritage in Lee County, although dwindling in number.

Grapevine's "Cross-Bar Hotel"

If you want to see how attitudes have changed about law-breakers in Texas, it is not necessary to visit the state's numerous "hanging trees" that were associated with the lawlessness of the Old West. All one has to do is visit the beautiful, history-packed, Tarrant County city of Grapevine, Texas. There, sitting on the northern fringes of the DFW Airport, one can inspect low-budget housing for those who ran afoul of the law in the early twentieth century. Standing on the city's historic Main Street as a warning beacon for all to see and as a concrete (literally) "word to the wise" is the Grapevine Calaboose which, incidentally, comes from the Spanish slang word for jail, "calabozo."

A fact sheet provided us by the Grapevine Historical Foundation tells us that in 1909 the Grapevine town council voted unanimously to build the community's first calaboose—town jail. Grapevine had previously relied on the Tarrant County sheriff to provide law enforcement. Founded in the 1850s, the town would now have its own lawman and jail. The council gave town marshal W.T. Bigbee authorization to construct the 8-foot by 10-foot by 8-foot concrete jail. In the same meeting, Marshal Bigbee was given $4.50 for the purchase of a pair of handcuffs. "It is supposed the marshal had his own gun." The marshal was offered $25 a month.

If its cramped size is not enough to be convincing of the locals' attitude toward wayward citizens and visitors, perhaps its accommodations will show how bereft of comfort it was! The calaboose, which was, no doubt, home to numerous rowdy cowboys in its day, was outfitted with a single iron cot, and a tarp covered its openings to keep out chilly winds. The fact sheet tells us that eventually these accommodations became inadequate to house even the

Built in 1909, the Grapevine calaboose was the community's first jail. The concrete structure measuring 8x10x8 feet was "home away from home" for numerous unruly cowboys. By 1953 the calaboose, with its single iron cot and tarp to cover the opening, keeping out cold winds, was no longer adequate to house prisoners and fell into ruin. (Photo by Bill Binnig)

occasional inebriated citizen and fell into ruin. It was not used much after 1953 to hold prisoners and was moved to the city's historic district to sit along with the city's other buildings of yesteryear.

Vintage News in North Texas

One sure way to revisit history is by reading the newspapers of yesteryear. Thanks to the Grapevine Heritage Foundation, we were able to scan a decades-old edition of that city's *Grapevine Sun*, which enabled us to reach back in time and glean a few stories that were newsworthy at the time. In some cases we found the news was not so different from today's. We found some that today we find almost laughable, while others were most horrific! We offer the following as examples of yesterday's noteworthy news:

The biggest headline grabber in the Easter Sunday April 1 edition of the *Grapevine Sun* involved the infamous Barrow gang. This story may well be burned in the memory of some of us today! The headlines read, "BONNIE AND CLYDE MURDER LOCAL POLICEMEN." That's right, policemen, plural! The story reminds us how "three motorcycle policemen were patrolling on Highway 114 west out of Grapevine. One officer, 24-year-old H. D. Murphy, was on his first day of official patrol duty. He was scheduled to be married in a few days to his 20-year-old fiancé in Alto, Texas." The officers saw a car parked on a side road. One officer rode ahead and the other two tagged behind. The first officer later noticed that the other two were not behind him. He returned and found them lying dead in the road. The two had decided to investigate.

A farmer sitting on his front porch was able to give an account as to what happened. "The two stopped, dis-

THE DAILY TIMES HERALD

CLYDE AND BONNIE DIE IN BARRAGE OF GUNFIRE FROM OFFICERS IN LOUISIANA

SLAIN AS SPEED TO HIDEOUT WATCHED BY TEXANS FOR WEEK

CLYDE, BONNIE PUT ON SPOT BY CRIME PAL

DALLASITES TAKE PART

Two Mothers Grieve In West Dallas for Dead Bandit and Moll

This May 23, 1934 edition of the Dallas Daily Times Herald reports the end of the Barrow gang with their slaying in a lawmen's ambush in Louisiana.

mounted, and with guns in holsters walked towards the parked car. When they got within twenty-five feet of the car a man and woman stepped out of the vehicle, each firing shotguns. Both officers fell, mortally wounded. The farmer said the woman walked calmly over to one officer on the ground and shot him again. Then she and the man got into the car and drove off." The farmer's eyewitness account linked Clyde Barrow and Bonnie Parker to the slayings.

Another headline from the police blotter, while not so dramatic, points out another item from days gone by: the simple headline "FILLING STATION ROBBED." Bearing the dateline "Grapevine, Feb. 21, 1935," the gist of the story is that during the commission of an armed robbery, which would be commonplace today, "the masked bandit took the cash from the cash register and gathered up the cigarettes and a slot machine from the counter, rushed to a waiting car and made off going west." We found it noteworthy that there was, at this time in Texas, "one-armed-bandits" openly in service in some businesses.

Another headline in the old newspaper would be ludicrous today, especially with Grapevine's sitting on the threshold of one of the world's busiest airports. The headline reads, "NINE-YEAR-OLD SEES FIRST AIRPLANE." The brief item tells us that "Thelma Daniels got quite a start the other day. She was working in a field with her father when she heard a noise overhead. She looked up and saw an airplane for the very first time!" The item tells how she was so surprised she kept looking up. She was plowing with a one-row mule. She heard her father shout at her, "Get off that one row!"

CAREER ENDED AT LAST

This newspaper photo of Clyde Barrow and his gun-moll, Bonnie Parker, appeared in the report of their deaths at the hands of Louisiana and Texas lawmen in Gibsland, Louisiana.

Perhaps it is important for us to be able to look back every now and then and learn what was important to those who preceded us. In doing so we are reminded of those things that have slipped through our collective memories!

"Buffalo Soldiers": from Cannon Fodder to Texas Heroes

It was not until the horrific carnage of the Civil War that American Negroes were permitted to serve in the regular U.S. Army. When it became evident that the fierce fighting was going to decimate the Union fighting forces, which were made up of white Americans, it was decided that Negro slaves would be accepted on a volunteer basis to serve in the U.S. Army. This, they reasoned, would save the lives of thousands of white American soldiers destined to be claimed by the ferocious fighting. The first black men accepted to fight alongside white soldiers were accepted literally as cannon fodder. Many white officers refused to command black troops, feeling them unequal to the task of soldiering. Before long the bravery showed by the black soldiers who died by the thousands as Confederate forces cut them down like a giant rapier was enough to mellow the opinions of white officers. Before the conflict was over, praise was being heaped on the blacks by all but the die-hard, race-conscious white officers. These first Negro soldiers performed in such a way their ability could no longer be doubted.

The Civil War laid the groundwork for some of Texas' most heroic and often unheralded heroes, those black troopers known as the "Buffalo Soldiers." During the Indian Wars between 1866 and 1891, the time of Texas' settlement toward its westward border, 10,000 blacks made up 20 percent of the cavalry and 10 percent of the entire

U.S. Army. They were nicknamed "Buffalo Soldiers" by the Indians because their matted, wooly hair resembled that of the buffalo. Having overcome the prejudices of their white counterparts, they were assigned to forts that had been established along the Texas western frontier to protect the mail route between San Antonio and El Paso and to protect travelers and settlers attempting to expand Texas' civilization westward.

Following the Civil War the United States formed two Cavalry Regiments, the Ninth and Tenth Cavalry. These units were made up of Negro soldiers who wanted to remain in the army after the Civil War. Their mission was to control hostile Indians who stood in the way of settlers invading the great plains.

Named for Jefferson Davis, secretary of war and later president of the Confederacy, Fort Davis in Jeff Davis County was established in 1854. It was abandoned by the Army during the Civil War. Buffalo Soldiers were sent to reoccupy it in 1867. The fighting prowess of the Buffalo Soldiers won the respect of whites and Indians, alike.

Index

W

Wagenhaeuser, Anton, 158
Waggoner Mansion, 171, 172
Waggoner, Dan, 170
Walker, Samuel, 60
Wallace, W.A.A. (Bigfoot), 59, 60
Washburn Tunnel, 124
Watson, Floyd A. "Dock," 129
Waxahachie, Texas, 87
Weidmann, Gus, 104
Wends, 195
West End, 157, 173
where the west begins, 127

whipping oaks, 89
white buffalo, 28, 29, 94, 107
"whizzed-by" cemetery, 147
Wichita Falls, 6
Wild Bunch, 102
world's richest acre, 113
world's littlest skyscraper, 7, 8

Y

Yates, Amigo, 20, 21

Z

Zufelt, Rhema, 88